Innovations in Activities for the Elderly

Proceedings of the 1984 National Association of Activity Professionals Convention

About the Editor

Jane D. Cook is an activity consultant and editor of *Scrapbook Pages,* a bi-monthly large print publication written primarily for shut-in elderly. Her experience in the long term care field began in 1971 when she was employed as an activity coordinator in a SNF/ICF facility in Falls Church, Virginia. After more than seven years in that position, she joined the staff of American Health Care Association, Washington, D.C., where she was staff representative for the Section of Activity Coordinators. While employed there she served as editor of *Sharing and Caring* and *Senior American.* She wrote several booklets relating to activities and volunteer training.

Mrs. Cook is a Liberal Arts graduate of Penn State University and has completed graduate level work in communications at American University, Washington, D.C. She has been trained as an instructor of the basic 36-hour course for activity coordinators and has assumed a role in teaching that course in several states. She currently is on the faculty of the Leisure and Aging Management School, sponsored annually by the University of Maryland and other groups interested in recreation for the elderly.

Mrs. Cook is Chairman of Education for the National Association of Activity Professionals and a charter member of that organization.

Innovations in Activities for the Elderly

Proceedings of the 1984 National Association of Activity Professionals Convention

Jane D. Cook
Editor

The Haworth Press
New York

Innovations in Activities for the Elderly: Proceedings of the 1984 National Association of Activity Professionals Convention has also been published as *Activities, Adaptation & Aging*, Volume 6, Number 3, Spring 1985.

The Haworth Press, Inc., 10 Alice Street, Binghamton, NY 13904–1580
EUROSPAN/Haworth, 3 Henrietta Street, London WC2E 8LU England

Library of Congress Cataloging in Publication Data

National Association of Activity Professionals (U.S.).
Convention (2nd : 1984 : Denver, Colo.)
Innovations in activities for the elderly.

"Has also been published as Activities, adaptation & aging, volume 6, number 3, spring 1985"—T.p. verso.
Includes bibliographies.
1. Aged—United States—Recreation—Congresses. 2. Aged—Institutional care—United States—Congresses. I. Cook, Jane. II. Title.
GV184.N29 1984 790.1'926 84-28996
ISBN 0-86656-389-X

Innovations in Activities for the Elderly

Activities, Adaptation & Aging
Volume 6, Number 3

CONTENTS

Innovations in Activities for the Elderly

Proceedings of the 1984 National Association of Activity Professionals Convention

FROM THE GUEST EDITOR

Activity programs in nursing homes and retirement homes are as broad in scope as life itself. What kinds of events will result in the greatest sense of satisfaction for the nursing home resident? Obviously, the answer to that depends on the individual resident. It is a great mistake to think of nursing home residents as a homogeneous group. The longer people live, the more unique they become. Obviously the widow of a mid-west farmer and the retired professor of microbiology will gain a real sense of satisfaction from quite varied activities. The activity coordinator is working with the most diverse population that exists.

What, then, does the activity professional want to learn and experience at an annual conference devoted to his field? It is difficult to find a subject area that has absolutely no relevance to activities. Some knowledge of the whole area of health, both physical and emotional, is vital to the activity coordinator who will carry out his role successfully. So, too, is an understanding of the gratification a person receives from learning new information and developing new skills, from helping others around him, from social interaction with friends his own age as well as those of different generations, from a spiritual relationship and sense of an Almighty presence.

To put together the program for the second annual convention of the National Association of Activity Professionals, we turned to the activity professionals themselves and asked, not so much what they wanted to learn, but rather what did they want to share with their colleagues. Responses ranged from information about specific programs and ideas to the theoretical rationale for those programs.

The content of this issue hints at the variety of topics that offer the activity coordinator concrete directions for programming, theoretical reasons for developing and refining such programming, and inspiration and refreshment necessary to return to his very creative and demanding job.

Those attending the convention in Mile-High Denver were urged via the conference theme, to "Shift into High in the Climb Upward." Many of the participants had traveled upward to Denver's altitude, but they had only to look to the westward horizon to see that they had not yet reached the top of the world. Inspiring snow-covered peaks held out the possibility of greater goals and the promise of greater achievements.

Experienced climbers shared their special successes with their colleagues. "Old-timers" pulled; "newcomers" pushed. Together they are responsible for the upward progress that characterizes this relatively new field. Convention attendees looked "Into Aging" and found some reasons why the population they serve deserves their best efforts. They considered "Environmental Press" and know that they play an extremely important part in maintaining that population's mental, emotional and physical fitness. They learned how others have challenged the elderly to continue living.

This volume serves as a more or less permanent record of the sharing that took place between creative dedicated professionals engaged in an ongoing struggle to retain or increase quality in the lifestyles of many elderly.

Jane D. Cook

Keynote Address

Edith M. Sherman

Thank you for asking me to address your second Annual Convention. My respect and admiration for each and every one of you is boundless. Your work, your devotion, your "hope" in the face of numerous odds against success—deserve the support of the entire community, deserve accolades of the highest order, and above all deserve increased financial remuneration! You are truly the *care-givers* of our society to the needy, the disabled, to those "who suffer."

THE SETTINGS IN WHICH YOU WORK

Your task is unique because of the setting in which you work—the institution. Just what does it mean to be institutionalized? A colleague of mine has taught a course at the University of Denver entitled "Total Institutions." In this course three institutions were included as being *total.* They are: (1) prisons, (2) hospitals, (3) universities.

What are the common denominators of these three institutions? What synonyms reflect the condition of persons living and working in them? Let me suggest the following list for your consideration: incarcerated, controlled, routinized, isolated, dependent, depersonalized, acquiescent, regulated.

All of these terms imply an enormous loss of one's basic humanness, identity, self respect, self image, control of one's environment and decision making capacity. Is it any wonder that persons so institutionalized suffer severe depression, feelings of self hatred, loss of personal esteem—all accompanied by anger and the inevitable question—why me?

Society must bear its share of guilt for its acceptance and extension of ugly stereotypes of the aging and the disabled. The famous psychological theory, "Each to each a looking glass, reflects the other that doth pass," can be readily seen in the negative ways

American society perceives the elderly and disabled, and in the endless ways in which we try to deny, avoid, avert, cover up the processes of aging in ourselves and those we love.

The ill and disabled elderly are often portrayed as unloved and unloving. This perception is a cultural one and reflects a *value system* that can and should be changed and reevaluated.

I often recall a tribute to the Chicana grandmother in San Luis, Colorado. She was 106 years old (perhaps the oldest person in our state) and the Denver Post covered her birthday celebration. Under the picture of her deeply wrinkled face and another of her aged hands with numerous age spots was the caption, "The serenity of Prima Suaza." There is no question that her beauty and serenity were in the eyes of her beholders in this ethnic community which has a different set of values.

GOALS OF THIS MEETING

The goals of this meeting as they are stated in your program are:

1. To gain knowledge
2. To share ideas
3. To improve programming
4. To renew enthusiasm

Let us address these hopes and aspirations as you start your second annual convention.

My own interest in activities for the frail/institutionalized was kindled on a study tour to Scandinavia sponsored by Columbia University in 1970. At a geriatric care center in Norway I observed the first dance class I had ever witnessed in such a facility. A young college student (physical education or dance major) with his recording machine and marvelous Scandinavian folk music was conducting in a group setting a *regular* dance class for all of the residents who could come or be brought by aides or activity directors to the sessions. Despite the fact that his class consisted of persons in beds that had been moved into the room, in wheelchairs, on walkers, using canes, the session was a dance class, not physical therapy.

The importance of the event to me was the impact such a class had upon the residents.

1. In a group setting, there was the opportunity for socialization with teacher, staff, and other residents.
2. A scheduled event gave the residents something to look forward to and plan for. This event was better than reality therapy because the days for dance class were anticipated with pleasure.
3. The change in routine increased the residents' awareness of time and relationships.
4. The music, dancing and humanities had a positive impact on the attitudes of the residents.

Aristotle's famous phrase, "Man (and woman) is by nature a social animal," cannot be stressed too much. Human beings need to remain social animals regardless of their age or physical condition. The opposite of socialization is solitary confinement. When it is used by some institutions, as is done so *wisely* at times, it inflicts the maximum degree of pain and suffering.

GOALS OF YOUR ASSOCIATION

The primary goal of activity professionals in their work environment could be summarized as the expansion of residents' and patients' physical and social life space that will contract if left to normal circumstances.

Four walls of one's room diminish the stimulation and interaction needed by all people. Intimacy with family members, close friends, and meaningful others is often lost. Social interaction with impersonal caretakers can be devastating.

The elderly do not lose their sexual needs. By that I mean a broad definition that includes touching, embracing, and stroking. Today there is a great emphasis on pet therapy, a kind of substitute for human closeness of a physical nature. One nursing home resident was heard to greet his family with, "Why don't you greet me like the dog does?"

Two examples of alternative programming to expand the life space for the elderly/disabled have recently come to my attention and I would like to share them with you.

Over the Hill Gang is a group of older skiers. The physical activity has proved to be almost a side benefit. Most people go just to achieve the companionship of others with similar interests. The group has expanded from skiing to hiking, swimming, surfing, etc.

Roadrunners is a program of field trips organized for residents and patients of chronic care facilities by a Denver priest. It began with 30 persons and one bus and has grown to its present size, 30 buses and 900 persons. Again, socialization is the biggest attraction, with change in routine and new experiences next in importance. When asked about how the project was financed, the Father replied with hands outstretched, "God provides."

IMPROVING PROGRAMMING WITH NEW IDEAS

Activity programs need to be beyond the arts/crafts/female-type activities that were prevalent in the early days of the activity coordinator. Too often the humanities are neglected. There is a wealth of material to be tapped in art, literature, history, music, government, law. Many a lively discussion can center around aspects of our culture, such as food, drink, entertainment, holidays, theater, the media, philosophy and values, travel.

The National Council on the Aging (NCOA) series entitled "Self Discovery Through the Humanities" offers a wide variety of resource material for developing such programs based on literature and art. Some examples of topics available include: "A Family Album," a look at the family in literature; "Words and Music," an introduction to American musical comedy; "The Heritage of the Future," current events and their importance to future generations; "Work in American History." These programs make use of positive reminiscence and life review techniques, of photographic review as well as personal and historical calendars.

Creative writing in the form of poetry or papers and newsletters written by residents themselves expand the life experiences of those we serve. Contests for such creative endeavors can offer motivation for those who are reluctant to try.

Short courses taught by universities are finding their way into senior housing developments, nursing homes, and senior centers. Residents themselves choose the courses. In one such experiment now funded by the Colorado Department of Higher Education, diplomas are given for work completed.

The Great Books series offered by the University of Chicago is another source of program ideas.

Open Enrollment in Colleges and Universities gives opportunity for life long learning. The dissertation of a doctoral student at the University of Denver recently contained comments on the impact of such enrollment. The English instructor wrote, "The Senior Citizen in my class on American literature, which as you know these days is nothing but 'sex and sin,' took to it like a duck to water."

Intergenerational projects, service/learning experiences of all types, help to destroy the artificial age-graded separation of the generations. The 1982 Oscar-winning documentary film "Close Harmony" illustrates the marvelous use of music to bring children together with people of their grandparents' generation.

Residents of nursing homes need to be incorporated into any and all of the local events that may be of interest to them. In 1983 15 or 20 residents from the Glen Valley Nursing Home in Glenwood Springs, Colorado, traveled 40 miles to attend a rehearsal of the famous Aspen Orchestra in Aspen, Colorado. The event represented the cooperative efforts of managers, staff, local service organizations, and the Music Associates of Aspen to make a treat available to institutionalized people. Involvement in local events is one way of overcoming the dissociation which happens to so many patients and creating a future worth looking forward to.

THE USE OF COMMUNITY RESOURCES

The provision of a well-rounded and challenging activity program cannot be the responsibility of one or two staff persons working alone. Community resources are available and are essential to the program.

(1) The Family. Where members of families exist and reside close to residents, they contribute an estimated 80 percent of the services to older family members. However, a goodly number of nursing home residents, especially women, are end-products of the depression years which left many females unmarried and childless.

Where family members are available, they can be extremely helpful to institutions and staff. As primary caregivers, however, they can become martyrs, overworked and abused. Many middle-aged women, daughters and daughters-in-law, are today working in the job-market and are sandwiched in between the teen-aged generations and the grandparent generations. They themselves may already be older and unable to care for the old-old, frail, at-risk generation.

(2) Volunteers. A great source of programming help if properly managed, volunteers need a Director of Volunteer Services if they are to be united into an organized, dependable, rewarded cadre of help that represents all ages. I personally believe that through a "Youth Corps" all young people should spend a year or two in social and community service programs. In that way they would become better acquainted with many segments of our population which are so readily overlooked or ignored.

Look to volunteer groups such as RSVP, Senior Aides, Senior Companions, Foster Grandparents, Teachers' Aides, Paralegal Workers, Church Groups, Auxiliaries, Candy-stripers, etc.

A word of warning is needed here. Don't confuse volunteer services, supplementary and auxiliary, with major programs that must be *sustained by society* and which result from life-long contributory taxes by almost every member of our society. I am referring to Social Security, Supplemental Security Income, Medicare, Medicaid, Aid to the Partially/Totally Disabled, Aid to the Blind, and the means tested programs for the poor *and* needy.

(3) Advocacy and Action-Oriented Programs. People who are old or ill or disabled need to have some feelings of control of their own lives. It is important for them to participate in political activity, to vote, to discuss current issues, to hear from their leaders, to join organizations that represent their interests.

In a recent *New York Times* article I read the following precepts for healthy aging:

1. Stay socially involved.
2. Remain mentally active.
3. Have a flexible personality.

It is important to avoid atrophy. Let the parts wear out rather than rust out from disuse.

In closing, let me tell you about an elderly woman who kept a positive attitude. She was overheard discussing retirement plans and options with her husband, saying, "If one of us dies, I'm going to Florida."

Interdisciplinary Teamwork

Sister Patricia Murphy

Who among us have not been swept up into the fever and excitement of the qualifiers and performances of the Olympics. Even from an armchair perspective, it is clear that each and every event is born in many layers of teamwork from a network of human support performance—an inter and multidisciplinary approach.

We long term care workers have our own Olympics on a daily basis and our success is dependent on our teamwork and our disciplinary relations. All our programming and care is intended to dovetail toward the meeting of our resident's special needs. Many of the "quality of life" needs are psycho-social and each department holds within its mandate the responsibility to meet these psycho-social needs through their specific service. We, whose departments revolve specifically around psycho-social needs, must be continually aware of the need to extend opportunities to all departments, to contribute to the design, implementation and evaluation of specific programs that meet psycho-social needs.

I would like to share the story of an activity professional whose relief couldn't seem to meet expectations. She felt she was the only one in the facility who really understood the needs of the residents and she couldn't figure out why she found herself planning and executing programs all by herself. She couldn't understand why residents weren't dressed and prepared for programs; why she was the sole transporter of residents; why the cook forgot the birthday cake; why hard work craft items were thrown out by housekeeping; why the activity coordinators' room was dirty from other programs; why medication nurses disturbed her programs by calling out names or saying loudly "swallow, swallow"; why residents were taken out of the middle of programs for their baths; why the van went home with

Sister Patricia Murphy is currently serving her second term as President of the National Association of Activity Professionals. She is the Corporate Director of Activities and Social Services for Beverly Enterprises, Pasadena, CA. "Sister Pat" earned her MA degree in Communication Arts from Loyola University of Los Angeles; is a published author, a lecturer and has been a TV host.

the administrator the week of the outing; why staff couldn't seem to be cajoled to come to programs unless they had food involved; why residents were uneasy with each other but warm and friendly to her; why residents resisted volunteers and kept telling her they really preferred her services; why volunteers were only interested as long as she worked with them. This activity professional had a difficult time doing the program she felt was so important because she ended up being all alone and this happened because she didn't make good use of the rest of the team.

Sometimes we feel activity professionals seem quite alone in meeting these psycho-social needs as though other departments are too busy or perhaps don't even care about what happens in their departments. We can go a long way toward changing this by seeing to it that we act as part of a team which offers many ways for all departments to meet resident's psycho-social needs. This attitude will contribute toward making the provisions of programming an administrative priority, an all staff responsibility, an interdisciplinary premise, and a program and service plan that functions seven days a week.

We might take a look at just who is the team we are part of. A mental check indicates administration, nursing, social services, housekeeping, maintenance, and clerical. However, there are other vital components to a team approach and they are consultants, residents, family, community services, community religious sector, community college, hospital discharge planners, senior art and education specialists, recreation and parks department and so forth.

The Social Services and Activities Department does provide one of the best vehicles for all members of the team to meet their need to participate in formal psycho-social programming. And, we do come prepared with more training slanted to design systems to meet psycho-social needs but we will never accomplish the scope, variety and leadership in our programming by ourselves.

What is the process of teamwork? First, there needs to be a personal and staff perception of your place on the team. Second, you need to utilize your current programs to educate, influence and cooperate with the rest of the team members. These areas are:

a. care plan meetings
b. department head meetings
c. in-services (let's specifically show why the programs we utilize in our departments are useful in meeting resident's needs)

d. resident council
e. family council
f. community forums

You already have within your own department many areas in which to collaborate in team planning:

a. Calendar planning that involves the whole staff, the Resident Council. All of our calendars should be reviewed by these components before they take formal and final shape so it needs to be done monthly as well as in an overall way on a yearly basis.
b. Program evaluation—We should do at least a quarterly program evaluation with the rest of the team so that they can get input to what they feel has been successful from their point of view.
c. Major event review—After each major event (e.g., National Nursing Home Week) the staff and members of the team should be asked for their evaluation of the event, what could be changed and what could be added.
d. Program participation by the rest of the team especially in the early a.m. and weekend programming. If we make it possible for other members of the interdisciplinary team to participate in a failsafe way in leadership positions we will give them the satisfaction of knowing just how important these programs are to our residents.
e. Program posting—Each nursing station, each department head station should be a calendar in easy view. Special programs should be posted in these areas when specific team participation is required.
f. Utilizing the staff to train volunteers will help the staff understand this part of our team and take some responsiblity for their successes.
g. The model set of teamwork among the social rehabilitation staff and volunteers, both resident, family and community will give the rest of the staff an idea of the benefits of interdisciplinary collaboration.

Most of us have experienced the pay-off of interdisciplinary teamwork usually after a big event that comes off successfully. We listen to the other staff talking excitedly about how one or the other residents did things they never expected were possible. We've seen these same residents perform that way before and we could be feeling rather smug that the experience taught something special to "them." But this should be a daily occurrence, not an exception and our own indefatigable efforts at being effective team members and consistent. Integrating the rest of the team into our program will help this experience to multiply.

The pay-off comes when:

—The whole staff recognizes that an activity is more successful when they actively participate.
—When nursing begs for an activity program of their own.
—When dietary wants to be in charge of the monthly birthday programming.
—When maintenance involves your men residents in a men's program.
—When housekeeping insists on giving a class in "personalizing" a resident's room.
—When the Administrator runs the new resident/family tea.
—When clerical gives a program on nursing home personal monies use.
—When the gardener makes sure some residents are involved.
—When Community Service asks for your expertise in meeting psycho-social needs and promises an exchange of resources.
—When the city Recreation and Parks Department asks when you'd like to use their van.
—When the surveyors ask if you would mind their taking your multi and interdisciplinary plan to other facilities.
—When families tell other prospective clients that your facility has all kinds of staff doing all kinds of interesting programs.
—When schools ask your residents to teach "aging" education.
—When universities choose our facility among many for field work because you train activity professionals for the long term future as well as today.

Both within the facility and outside the facility, there is great need for a better understanding of the capabilities of our "disabled" residents and what they can contribute to the well being of those who serve them and the community from which they came. We have the opportunity to extend the network of the resident, the staff and the facility when we educate, learn from, utilize and promote a multi-interdisciplinary approach in long term care services.

Into Aging—A Simulation Game

Joanne Williams

While aging is something that all of us do from the moment we are born until we die, it still is largely a taboo topic in the United States. Sex, with all its ramifications, is a topic that is quite all right for discussion by the old and young in almost any context. Death, too, is an acceptable topic in workshops on death and dying, in religious sectors and in special courses in health sciences. But aging is rarely acceptable as a topic; it is still largely avoided.

The consequences of this avoidance is that less is known about the normal aspects of the process of aging, and less enlightened policies and health planning for the aged are produced.

"Into Aging" is a vehicle whereby our societal avoidance of issues confronting those people over 65 years of age is immediately challenged. In our largely age-graded society, it is fairly easy to avoid interchange with those not in a particular age group. This game creates a familiarity and awareness of issues and problems of aging.

"Into Aging" is a very well researched simulation game. Its authors painstakingly consulted the literature for data, statistics, theories and other types of materials to aid them in the formulation of the game. The likelihood of certain events in the game is carefully tied to the probability of the same events in the real world.

When you play "Into Aging," you will find that you emerge a much changed individual. It will no longer be possible for you to ignore your own aging process or to avoid the aged around you without at least a twinge of guilt. "Into Aging" is a powerful instrument. It serves not to teach content in the field of gerontology per se but to sensitize the player to areas of interest and concern which previously had not been within their focal awareness.

The game is a microcosmic experience intended to dramatize cer-

Joanne Williams, author, lecturer, and consulting editor with Potentials Development for Health and Aging Services, has served as an activity coordinator in both a skilled nursing facility and in a retirement residence. She is a member of the Board of Trustees of NAAP.

tain attitudes and beliefs underlying society's way of dealing with the elderly. Many aspects of life were introduced into the subject matter for scrutinization. What follows is a brief overview of some of the more common situations of the elderly as well as how they become problems and affect stereotyping.

Because of the dynamic social structure in which humans exist, the individual is continually influencing and being influenced by the environment. This interaction begins at conception and progresses to death. During the process of growing, we monitor the way we are received by the environment and adjust our behavior to achieve the response we expect to be appropriate. The myth that old people are static and unchanging is thus disproved. The elderly pick up cues about what is expected from them in the way of behavior, and may conform to stereotypes instead of to their own expression of self. So to a great extent, the way we see the elderly may well be a reflection of our own attitudes about them.

The perceptual faculties such as sight, smell, taste, hearing and touch are all subject to impairment due to natural changes. These perceptual changes become more important when the individual interacts with others. Humans rely heavily on verbal communication. One's perceptual framework or beliefs about aging leads him to interpret difficulties and changes as being due to "senility" rather than normal deficits in the senses that in some cases can be corrected.

Each player in the game receives a set of instructions and is given a few minutes to read this before play commences. This provides the rules to be followed and goal to be achieved. The game is designed to allow participants to experience problems which many old people face in our society today.

When the game is over, players discuss their experiences and feelings. As part of the game, they assume the identities they see themselves as having when old, thereby investing personal values into the game. Players share their identities and proceed to three tables, set up to represent three modes of living: independent, semi-dependent, and dependent. Each table has a stack of Life-Event cards. The deck is stacked with odds against the players, forcing them into a dependent life style. The exercise which must be done to obtain an income is difficult, signifying the financial problems old people have. The end result is that players experience the loss of many valued objects, including their identity, and becoming increasingly dependent, isolated, and powerless.

A debriefing period after the game is essential because, although "Into Aging" is a game, it is not necessarily fun. It is a learning tool. Players are encouraged to discuss their experiences and how these problems can be dealt with positively. Hopefully, the player will develop and practice skills in recognizing myths and stereotypes and creating change.

The following are personal impressions and observations from having presented this workshop several times in California. The game is negatively oriented so chances of winning are slim. Strong, honest, life-loving players have found themselves altering behavioral patterns in order to survive with dignity. Occasionally a player will cheat or lie or steal or hide in order to retain his meager posessions or identity. As negative circumstances begin to catapult, even the most enthusiastic, optimistic player may choose suicide because the future appears hopeless.

In debriefing, feelings have come out strong, voices have become loud and competitive as anger was expressed over the attitudes about aging. Resentment over the losses has been a major issue, particularly when the player considered him/herself still capable of decision-making and limited control.

Having expressed feelings, players are allowed to "rewrite" game event cards in a more positive, winning manner. They discuss how changes can be made in their facilities, with their clients, in their own families, to alter perceptions of aging and gain insight. Questionnaires following the game reveal negative patterns players have become trapped in. New awareness as a result of playing "Into Aging" has sent participants away dedicated to changing their own perception and that of society within their reach.

Networking: How to Use What You've Got to Get More of What You Want

Jacqueline M. Bean

Networking: that's an "in" term for the decade, and for good reasons. It's the key to taking all the problems you encounter in your professional walk and plugging them into the people you know, so the doors will open for you—doors to solutions.

When you hear the word "networking," what do you think? Does that word hold any special meaning for you? If you think of contacts and how to develop them, you have a good idea of networking. If you picture support systems for information, advice and encouragement, you're on the right track. After reading the opening to Mary Scott Welch's book, *Networking,* one woman stated, "It's like a page full of little dots, with lines drawn every which way, connecting those dots."

Each person has his own private interpretation of the definition of the word. Each one has his own dynamic way of applying that definition. And everyone has his own personal reasons for using the networking concept. The important point is that networking is a process that helps people achieve their own goals.

In trying to achieve my own personal and professional goals, I first began realizing the power behind the network concept. It began with a project and a commitment to work with the elderly in convalescent settings. As with any project with high goals, my project brought me my share of pre-completion anxieties.

In the midst of a project, do you ever get the feeling of being overwhelmed? In working with the elderly, I did. I began seeing myself in the place of my residents.

Jacqueline M. Bean is a lecturer and editor of *Geri-Active Exchange*, with experience as an activity coordinator in long term care. Her varied background includes experience in drama, radio, music therapy, and public relations.

I am really worried about something. You see, I am a "baby boom" baby. That made things ever so exciting while we "baby boomers" were in high school and college, but the pressure is beginning to set in. While we went through our twenties and thirties, we began to realize what it meant to have just a little bit too many of us, and not enough of everyone else. The squeeze was on for housing and some commodities.

The population is getting top-heavy. While the median age in this country used to be young enough to make this a teen-oriented society, it is now edging toward forty. Our society is maturing. You can see it in the ads that cater to those over thirty and over forty. Products made especially for "hair over forty," Levis cut just a little bit wider than when we were teens.

We baby boomers will have plenty of company as we go through the "crisis years" of middle age. Fine; we can be sociable. But what happens when the median age slips closer to 50? I realize there will always be younger folks to pull the cumulative demographic aging effect back down, but what happens when the baby boomers reach 60 . . . 70 . . . 80?

Those who reside in nursing homes at this time are just a small percentage of the general population. And yet we struggle to keep up that steady quantity and quality of programs for our current residents. Will our innovations, plans and funding keep up an adequate pace so that the demand will be met when the baby boomers hit convalescent age?

Remember when the baby boomers hit school age? There was a sudden awakening to the need for quality education: build schools, train better teachers, pay teachers better salaries. By the time society was finally prepared to meet the onslaught, the baby boomers were slipping into their caps and gowns for the graduation ceremony. By then there were all those modern facilities, manned by excellently trained teachers who faced nearly empty classrooms. Sorry, Mom and Dad, your tax dollars did the trick, but too late!

What will happen in the year 2020? Baby boomers will turn seventy. Will American society wait until the crisis time to panic over potential gross lack of care for their elderly? Our programs may work now, given today's ratios and demographic spreads. But what about quality care in the future? We have to start building towards that program now.

Everyone is familiar with the people/time squeezes an activity coordinator experiences at times. That is like an experience I had a few years ago. I got this terrific idea for a new project at my facility. I decided to devise a system of hand signals that aphasaic stroke victims could use in order to communicate basic needs. I began teaching signs, modified from Standard American Sign Language. I taught the aides. I taught the entire nursing staff. Together, we were planning to work patiently and regularly with five to ten selected residents.

And then came crafts. And bingo. And music. And visiting time. And meetings. And paperwork. And the project lost the persistent effort it needed to stay alive. I dropped it. And I regretted it.

Later I learned how I could have handled the situation in a different manner. Instead of depending solely on paid staff, already overburdened with daily routine, I could have devised a new kind of plan. This was a plan I discovered through research for our state's professional council.

One day I was reading some information on taxes and the IRS and organizations. I ran across a phrase familiar to many of you: tax exempt non-profit corporation. I had known about those types of groups for years. But this day, I let my mind wander. I started thinking, "What if . . . "

What if I still could do my sign language project?

What if I could find funding for my idea and put it into a pilot project, with additional paid personnel?

What if all this could be done under the sponsorship of my state organization?

What if my state organization became a tax exempt non-profit corporation?

I began researching everything I could find on non-profit agencies . . . foundations . . . writing grants . . . fund raising. This turned up an enormous amount of data that boiled down to one fact. My idea, while fantastic, was going to need a lot of groundwork. In order to be prepared for the project, my main concern needed to be network building.

In order to make a project workable, you must first consider some things. Developing a project is like making a sandwich. Both have five basic elements. In making a sandwich, you grab a piece of bread, slap some mayo on it, follow that by some meat, then another slice of bread and mayo. Project-building involves investigation, identification of needs, network building, information gathering and dissemination, and development of resources. Five elements: and, like the sandwich, it is what is in the middle that counts. It's the meat that gives you muscle. It's the well-planned network that will insure your project's success.

Five steps: investigation, identification, networking, promotion and developing resources. The beginning and ending are easy. You already know what to do to invent creative projects. It's the middle step—networking—that demands extra attention.

So, how to build a network? How do you meet people? How do you plug them into your project? Consider the idea of influence.

Everyone has a sphere of influence. You need to let yours work for you. Visualize the impact of your sphere of influence. For a moment, in your mind's eye, picture yourself at the edge of a country pond, poised and ready to toss a pebble into the water. As the splash subsides, little ripples form where the pebble entered the water. Those ripples gradually expand, stretching out to reach to the very shores of that pond. Those ripples are like your sphere of influence.

Now, how do you make that sphere of influence work for you? Take another imaginary trip back to that country pond, only this time bring along a friend. You stand at one end of the pond, and your friend walks to the other end. Together you pick up pebbles, and simultaneously toss them into the water. As they hit the pond's surface, watch those ripples. Starting small, each pebble's impression on the water gradually radiates outward. At one point, the ripples from your pebble and those of your friend's intersect. At that point, you have illustrated a working network system. Your spheres of influence intersect.

The question arises: How far can your network reach? Theoretically, this could stretch on forever. To get a definite idea of your personal sphere of influence at this point, try an exercise. Take a piece of blank binder paper and a pen. We are going to organize your acquaintances through a technique called patterning.

First, in the center of the page, write the word "me." Draw a small circle around this word. Then, think of the various roles you play in your daily routine. You may be a volunteer, or a mother, or a supervisor. You may claim all of these titles and more. For each descriptive title of the aspects of your life, draw a line radiating out from the center word, like spokes on a wheel. Label each line with a title. Then, subdivide by listing descriptive tasks you fulfill. For instance, under the title volunteer, you may have three branches labeled political campaign, den mother and Red Cross. For the final step, begin filling in names of those you work with in each of those descriptive capacities. You then have a diagram of not only the areas in which you exercise your sphere of influence, but the people you influence regularly, as well.

This influence is important as a key element of networking. Spheres of influence are forever expanding. People are interfaced in a dynamic way as a method of goal accomplishment. In networking, there are four basic possibilities of operation. I may meet you, and we develop an acquaintance based on professional ties. In the course of my work, I may meet Mrs. X, whom I refer to you because she may need your assistance. Or you may refer me to a Mr. Y, who has the perfect idea for a project I'm tackling. Finally, you and I are careful to re-establish mutual ties on a regular basis.

In each of these four instances of networking, the contacts are made to help or give help to professionals, not only in activities, but in all fields and occupations. This becomes especially important when a project you are working on suddenly needs advice from an accountant or support from a politician. If you have developed and enlarged your sphere of influence, offering your own expertise where possible, it is like money in a savings account. What you do will come back to you through the networking endeavor.

Building a network is a task to be taken seriously. No matter how great your memory, keep everything on paper when it comes to remembering who your contacts are and why they are important. It is a good idea to develop a card file system in duplicate—filing each entry by name, alphabetically, and by a code system listing specializations, such as law, the media, or business. On each card, be sure to include room for the person's name, address, phone number, comments on areas of personal interest and professional affiliations. On the bottom of the card, or on the back, leave a good portion of space for record keeping on each meeting or contact, promises made and any other information to refresh your memory on the last mutual contact.

While networking is often used on a personal basis, the concept of networking can also be applied on a group basis. This becomes clear when you consider that each organization you are affiliated with is made up of individual members. These individuals all have their own spheres of influence. Why let your members be selfish? Give them the opportunity to share the wealth of their individual networks. Print up a questionnaire to help your members share information on their networks. This may prove valuable to you at a later time.

Networking skills are people-meeting skills. Sometimes people hesitate to expand their networks because they are apprehensive when it comes to making new acquaintances, especially those who will be asked to do a favor. And yet this skill is vital to professional self-improvement. If you feel like you need some moral support before embarking on a network-expanding project, try the following exercises with some friends or a group like your regional activity coordinators' organization.

To practice verbally putting your best foot forward (not in your mouth): have group sit in a circle. Round-robin, have each person take a turn at repeating and completing this statement: "I feel I am a successful Activity Coordinator because . . . " One by one, the participants will feel a growing confidence in their own unique skills.

To practice giving a verbal, concise description of your profession to new acquaintances, try this round-robin exercise using a moderator. The challenge is, in 25 words or less, to answer a "stranger from outer space" (the moderator) who has just asked you, "What do you do?" Don't take any stock phrases for granted, for the "alien" moderator's task is to constantly interject comments like "LTC? What's that?" Remember, your moderator is from outer space. Once you provide him or her (or it?) with a satisfying and concise description of your profession, you can be sure you will be amply prepared to take on the world and other humans like yourself.

To develop listening, divide into pairs. One person in each pair will begin telling the partner about a significant occurrence or project that gave that person satisfaction. The listening partner is allowed only a few minutes to hear the story before all partners have to split up and find new partners. At this point, the old listeners become the new speakers, telling about the story just told by the former partner. At the end of the session, have a few people share the stories of most interest with the group as a whole. Note how well the listener remembered details, and which story lines *helped* a listener remember the best.

Armed with records of your sphere of influence, current contacts, and with a good deal of confidence-building under your belt, you are ready to become an avid networker. The last point is really a question. Why are you, personally, interested in networking? What reason was there for you to develop the technique? In the beginning of this article, it was pointed out that network building is part of a process, the muscle of planning a successful project, no matter what the topic at hand. But what about you, personally? What is *your* current project?

Sit down for a minute and evaluate your current professional goals. What is your current project? List your objectives. Decide what type of people you need to meet. Review your evaluation of your present network to determine the network you will need to obtain your goal. Set a schedule to help you meet all the new people you will need to contact for your project. And constantly re-evaluate your plans and goals. Pace yourself for success.

Remember—no one likes to say ''no''; everyone likes to give advice. Keep others interested in what you are doing. Remember why you are networking. You want to receive input from successful people in their fields. You want to provide fellow professionals with a mutual support system. You want to advance your cause (and your career). You continually want to meet role models as a means of educational outreach. And you are building your network as a means of developing your current project. You are using what you have (your influence) to get what you want. You are utilizing your network to achieve your professional goals.

The Difference an Idea Makes: The Art of Brainstorming

Kimberly Chaffin

On a scale of ''1'' to ''10,'' where would you rate the importance in your position of new ideas and the ability to solve problems?

1 2 3 4 5 6 7 8 9 10

If most of you said ''10,'' my next question would be where would you rate yourself in possessing the ability to stimulate new ideas and solve problems?

1 2 3 4 5 6 7 8 9 10

Every person in this room possesses a vast resource of creative ideas, talents, and impressions of the world. Much of this remains untapped because the skills and confidence are lacking to bring them to the surface.

Today in this session you will learn the art and importance of brainstorming. ''Brainstorm'' as defined by The American Heritage Dictionary is a sudden, clever, whimsical, or foolish idea. To expand that, brainstorming is an orderly strategy in which problems can be worked out. Mastering the skills of brainstorming guarantees you the chance to develop new ideas, solve complex problems, and add whole new dimensions to your job.

Brainstorming is a method of creative thinking. The basic ingredient in any form of brainstorming is Osborn's four rules.

1. Criticism is ruled out.
2. Free-wheeling is welcomed. The wilder the idea the better.
3. Quantity is wanted.

Kimberly Chaffin is activity coordinator at Flannery's Nursing Home, Portsmouth, Ohio. She also serves as coordinator of a local Alzheimer's Support Group. She holds a BS degree in Consumer Services from Miami (Ohio) University. In 1983 Ms. Chaffin was listed among the Outstanding Young Women of the Year.

References from *Brainstorming* by Charles Clark, Doubleday & Company. 1958.

4. Combination and improvement are sought. Participants should suggest how ideas might be combined into better ideas.

To begin any brainstorming session one must first choose the problem to be attacked. There are two basic types of questions. The first, a *steam-shovel* question is very broad and general. For example: how can I enhance the public image of the nursing home? The problem with this type of question is that it is so broad that stimulating workable ideas from it would be difficult. Enhance the public image for whom? What would be the target audience?

A *spade* question digs into the problem. Work to establish a question that is worded in the shortest possible fashion but is limited. A question is limited by asking for who, when, where, and by whom. For example: how can the activity department enhance communication between relatives and residents? Could this question be even more limited? (during holidays?)

It is important that each member in the brainstorming session should know the four basic rules. There should be one leader of the session and one person to write the ideas down. There are certain phrases which should be ruled out by everyone participating. They are "killer phrases."

We've never done that before.
It won't work.
We haven't the time.
We haven't the manpower.
It's not in the budget.
We've tried that before.
We're not ready for it yet.
All right in theory, but can you put it into practice?
Too academic.
What will the customers think?
Somebody would have suggested it before if it were any good.
Too modern.
Too old-fashioned.
Let's discuss it at some other time.
You don't understand the problem.
We're too small for that.
We're too big for that.
We have too many projects now.
It's been the same for twenty years, so it must be good.

What bubble head thought that up?
I just know it won't work.
Let's form a committee.
Let's think it over for awhile.
That's not our problem.
Don't move too fast.
Why something new now?
Let's wait and see.
Here we go again.
I don't see the connection.
Nuts!
Sounds good, but I don't think it will work.
It's not in the plan.
No regulations covering it.
We've never used that approach before.
It'll mean more work.
It's not our responsibility.
It's too early.
It's too late.
It will offend.
It won't pan out.
Our people won't accept it.

Something just as negative as the "killer phrase" is the person who is apologetic about his own idea. Do you see yourself in any of these "self killer phrases?"

This may not be applicable but . . .
This may not work, but . . .
It isn't clear if we need this, but . . .
I don't know if we have the money, but . . .
It may be a dead end, but . . .
Would it hurt if we did?
Do you suppose it would be possible?
It may take a long time, but . . .
You probably have ideas about this too, but . . .
This may not be the right time, but . . .
This idea seems useless, but . . .
I'm not too familiar with this, but . . .
This may be too expensive, but . . .
You'll probably laugh but . . .

I haven't thought this one through, but . . .
It may not be important, but . . .
Joe doesn't agree with me but . . .
I realize this doesn't solve the problem, but . . .
If I'm out of line, correct me . . .

Don't be afraid to hitch hike on someone else's ideas. There should be no hesitation to speak out. Ideas should be punchy and quick. Ideas should not be sold, defended, or attacked. They are merely tossed on the table and jotted down. You are not trying to evaluate them; simply rush on to the next one.

A SAMPLE SESSION

Now we will test your brainstorming skills. Break up into groups of ten. Elect one person to take notes and one person to act as chairman to help identify the problem. You have 10 minutes to come up with the most ideas which solve this problem. How can activity directors improve communication between relatives and residents? You may reword the question or make it more specific if you wish.

SESSION FOLLOW-UP

1. Which group came up with the most ideas?
2. What problems did you encounter while you were brainstorming?
3. Was it difficult not to judge an idea?

The storm is over. Your list is full of ideas and where do you go from there? Ideas can't be hoarded. They are only considered valuable when they are turned into something (action, products, services, beliefs).

To make sure you have collected every possible idea, give everyone 24 hours to add other ideas to the list. Then let the list rest for a couple of days before sorting the ideas into three categories.

1. Hot ideas that can be tried almost immediately
2. Those which need long range planning
3. Those which are obviously unusable

Remain as open minded as possible. The 10 most workable ideas are the ones to be saved.

Selling your ideas to your facility is the next crucial step. Most people spend 95% of their energy thinking up new ideas and only 5% thinking about what to do with them. One ought to spend a third of the time putting his ideas to work. How does your administrator usually react to new ideas? Does he inhibit you by his attitudes? To sell someone else you should:

1. Appeal to their motives. How will your idea enhance their job?
2. Provide assurances, show them there is a need for it, a demand for it. That it won't increase their workload!
3. Have the idea well thought out and prepared.
4. If they begin to see advantages, let them add to the idea and feel that it is their own.

Individual brainstorming incorporates the same techniques as listed above but includes these steps:

1. Establish a good spade question.
2. Write down all the ideas that come to your head.

Brainstorming alone lacks the stimulation of other people, but it is possible to get ideas from many places. Reading magazines, walking the floors of the facility, spending hours in a library, looking at the problem in a new way. You can brainstorm anywhere. Now try your hand at some solo brainstorming.

The question: How can I celebrate my next birthday? Remember, there are no limits to money, time or distance. Write down all the possible answers to this question that come to your head.

Problems seemingly insoluble, irritating, frustrating, aggravating, frightening are the birthplace of new ideas. Duncan Hines was a printing salesman who had a hard time finding places to eat while he was traveling his territory. He sent out Christmas cards to friends recommending good places to eat. It became his career.

What problems exist in your facility which might be solved by a few new ideas? Think of an ideal workplace to you. That should produce many potential ideas. The facility I work in is an old mansion. It has winding staircases, a basement dining room and no activity room. These given situations leave me plenty of opportunities to develop ideas for adapting the activity program.

There are all sorts of ways to force yourself into working on those new ideas. Answer the following question: What would you gain if you could think of more ideas?

Now is the time to conceive ideas, and now is the right time to do something about them. First, brainstorm ways to make your job more rewarding and challenging. Then start putting them in action.

Residents in the Giving Role

Joan Betzold

Intergenerational activities have long been recognized as being of great benefit to all involved. The elderly have an opportunity to share their life experiences and be close to the freshness, fun and enthusiasm of youth. On the other hand, youngsters learn to appreciate, respect and understand, as well as benefit from the aging process. With this in mind, as Activity Director at Manor Care Rossville (Maryland) I began my search for intergenerational opportunities for the residents.

I presented my ideas to the Resident's Council. The vast majority of the residents were extremely excited about them. Many of their grandchildren and great-grandchildren are not allowed to visit due to what is conceived by family members as an "unhealthy" environment.

After many inquiries, I finally located a local Tiny Tot Center in White Marsh, Maryland. The school was owned and operated by the Baltimore Department of Parks and Recreation, with volunteer help by mothers. After much convincing, the Tiny Tot coordinator gave me permission to attend the registration meeting and plead my case. I took four Resident Council members to the meeting, introduced myself, and gave them the floor. By the time they finished their individual appeals to the parents, everyone in the room was in tears. They gave the residents a standing ovation and we were in!

The program was designed to get the tots into the facility, have some type of mutually interesting experience and the opportunity for sharing and interaction. The second Wednesday of every month at lunch time was chosen. Tots arrived with parents and teacher and "picknicked" on sheets on the dining room floor with the residents. The Dietary Department provided tot-like meals, i.e., peanut butter

---

Joan Betzold is Quality Assurance Manager for Activities, Manor Healthcare Corporation. Before accepting that position she was activity coordinator for the Manor Care facility in Rossville, Maryland. She received her BS degree in Therapeutic Recreation from the University of Maryland and is currently completing work for her Master's Degree in Rehabilitative Counseling.

and jelly sandwiches, hot dogs, cheese sandwiches, sloppy joes, etc. After lunch, entertainment was provided for all to enjoy.

Entertainment was tricky! Getting something that interested a population that ranged in age from 2 to 102 was a definite challenge. We experimented. Local resources were delighted to come in without charge. Some programs were successful and some weren't. Some extremely successful ideas include:

—American Indian dancers' demonstration and explanation of traditional dances
—Baltimore County Canine Division Policemen's demonstration of attack by police dogs
—Puppet shows
—Clown/magician show
—Baltimore Zoo slide show and touching display
—Judo/Karate demonstration
—Baltimore County Fire Department fire safety program. (Tots were allowed to try on coats, boots, etc.)
—American Flag history demonstration by the American Legion
—Santa (a resident) visit with distribution of gifts
—Pet Store (told how to take care of and let tots touch common pets, i.e., gerbils, guinea pigs, rabbits, cats)
—Doll show provided by the local doll hospital
—Kite show (local kite club brought slides and helped tots make their own kites)
—Baltimore Orioles player Al Bumbry talked and signed autographs. The team mascot, the Oriole Bird, accompanied him.
—Balloon release
—Mr. Do Bee from the TV show, Romper Room
—Balloon sculpture
—Baltimore Colts player Jimmy Moore talked and signed autographs
—National Nutrition Week program in March, featuring local food producers' mascots. Baron Von Esskay did a magic show; Green Spring Dairy Cow and Dairy Princess gave out cow erasers, coloring books, pencils, chocolate milk; Twinkie the Kid gave out Twinkies.
—Beekeeper showed an observation hive and offered tastes of different flavors of honey.
—Pinata filled with candy

EARLY VISITS

Initially staff, residents, parents, and tots were apprehensive. Tots cried and would not eat nor leave their parents. I decided I would try the exchange for a certain period of time and if the situation didn't improve, I would chalk it up for a good try. Improvement was dramatic! After two months, tots were sitting on residents' laps, giving out kisses. They even visited between luncheons.

The program continued to grow and flourish with both tots and residents taking more and more interest in each other. Soon residents were paying for the tots' meals out of the Resident's Council Treasury and preparing the meals themselves. By the end of the first year, the Council decided to present the Tot School with children's exercise records to thank them for coming and to show how much they loved them! I surmised the program was a success!

A RESIDENT-BUILT SURPRISE

As a formality, we again attended the next registration meeting that summer and the program had a firm foundation. During the summer, the Council discussed a big surprise project to give to the tots the following spring—something special. Many ideas were proposed. Finally the Council decided to construct a playhouse for the school.

The instructor of our Basic Woodworking for the Senior Adult course, offered through Essex Community College, was consulted on the project. Estimated cost was $400. That was all the information the residents needed. They got busy with raffles, bake sales, balloon releases and other money-making projects.

The plans were found, lumber and supplies purchased, and the work began under the instructor's supervision. Woodworking class worked on the house twice a week starting in October. As the pieces grew in size and number, an area in the nursing home's main dining room was sectioned off with sheets from ceiling to floor. The secret steadily grew.

The Council was very concerned about the authenticity, safety and durability of the house. The price of the house increased as we added real shingles, indoor-outdoor carpet, plexi-glass workable windows, etc. These raised the price to about $525.

The final touch was a hand-stenciled sign over the door:

Built and Donated by the
Residents of
Manor Care Rossville
May 14, 1980

The day of the unveiling arrived. Baltimore County Public Library heard about the secret and decided to film it for their "Generation" Series about elderly in the Baltimore area. The cameras and crew were set up, lunch was ready, and the presentation planned. The entire nursing facility was ecstatic.

The Council members moved into their positions. After a few short speeches, the sheets were raised. I remember the air as being still and everyone just taking a moment to enjoy the accomplishment and the outstanding workmanship, love and pride that was evident to all. That moment passed, as all 50 tots dashed for the house and played and screamed for over an hour, to the delight of the residents. Later, as the house was being loaded for transport to the tot center, a little boy cried and screamed, "You can't take my house!"

The Manor Care Rossville Tot House is permanently part of the Tot Center, the movie is permanently on file in Baltimore County Public Library, and the tot program is permanently part of Manor Care Rossville. It was a huge undertaking. Many times I doubted both my sanity for initiating it and our ability to complete it. The project pulled all the residents, volunteers, staff and families together. It is a treasured memory of the residents, and we show "Generations" every once in awhile to refresh that memory.

SPEAKER'S BUREAU

Another intergenerational activity that was extremely successful at Manor Care Rossville was the Resident's Speaker's Bureau.

As the Activity Director, I have oriented and "hired" many teenage volunteers. It has been fascinating over the years to watch the relationships develop between the elderly nursing home residents and the teen volunteers. More than any other age group, teenagers have demonstrated an intense interest in and involvement with the elderly. It continually amazes me every time I see a teenager adopt, in a completely accepting manner, a very confused resident who displays bizarre behavior.

These volunteers provide an in-facility outlet for the elderly to share their life experiences. I have long felt that even though a large number of teenagers interact with the nursing home residents, there is virtually a limitless number of teenagers that are never given that opportunity. The schools harbor the largest amount of this age group.

With this in mind, I literally set up a crusade to get a program going in the area schools. I initially contacted teachers that I was well acquainted with through the work study program. The teachers passived my inquiries with, "Yes, it sounds like a good idea. We'll work on it." That was the last I heard about it.

Finally, after working with them for another year, I began to exert pressure. The underlying message communicated was that we try my idea or they would lose their job site at the nursing center. As a result, Manor Care Rossville founded its Speaker's Bureau in the fall of 1980.

The first speaking engagement was in a work study class at Chesapeake Senior High; the topic, "Home Remedies and Superstitions." The residents were so excited to go. Three ladies volunteered to speak at the first session. The teachers were patient but dubious about the success. The tenth grade students were spellbound. They listened very intently, stayed awake and asked questions galore! Mr. Carroll, the teacher, let the students stay after the bell rang to continue the discussion but finally made them go to their next class.

As a result of the first encounter, the word spread like wild fire through the school and school district. The Student Council appointed a student coordinator to accept inquiries of times available and topics and to coordinate them with residents. I coordinated the transportation.

The program spread to six Baltimore County Junior and Senior High Schools. The response was amazing! Students begged to have the Speaker's Bureau visit their classes. Students stopped residents in the halls on the way to class—kissed, hugged and really made them feel special.

Several appointments were made every week. Some engagements lasted for several class periods. Topics included World War I, World War II, Growing Old, Women in the Working World, Immigration, What is a Fulfilling Life?, Motherhood, Death and Dying, Nazi Germany, as well as many others.

As a result of the Speaker's Bureau, a resident from the nursing center was invited to spend the day at Chesapeake Senior High. She went from class to class and was treated like one of the students, even given a bus ride home. After several years, the Baltimore County Public Library was convinced the program was going to survive and visisted one of the Speaker's Bureau sessions. They filmed another of their ''Generations'' series, which is available to all Baltimore County Public library patrons.

Interaction between the schools and the nursing center has continued to grow and flourish even today.

The bottom line is that intergenerational activities are terrific. Be patient and do a lot of public relations with your staff, families, tots and residents to get it going. But don't stop there. Use it as a starting point for something even bigger.

Making Connections Between the School System and the Nursing Home

Ruth Perschbacher

Activity programs in the long-term care setting serve a diverse population of elderly. The abilities, interests, and needs of this group vary widely. They frequently have dissimilar religious and social backgrounds. In order to meet this challenge, activity programs must combine resources with community settings. Intergenerational programs which utilize the educational system are examples of this resource sharing.

There are many potential advantages to using the public and private school system as resources for intergenerational programs. The school environment is relatively stable with regard to personnel, location, and scheduling. Operating the program with the same teacher and students over a period of time will provide consistency. The activities can be structured to meet objectives of the school as well as the nursing home. Additional grade levels within the school are resources for possible expansion. As the benefits to the students become evident, their parents are likely to promote the program. The school board and parent-teacher organizations may also become a support network for continuation and further development.

Most school systems will become involved in intergenerational programs for either the educational benefits or for service-oriented goals. Before contacting the school, the activity professional should understand the implications of intergenerational programs to both education and service. In education-oriented programs, the nursing home residents can utilize their knowledge and experience to teach oral history (Perschbacher, 1984), foreign languages (Laufer and

---

Ruth Perschbacher is currently employed at Hillhaven Rehabilitation and Convalescent Center, Asheville, North Carolina. She earned bachelor's degrees in music education and music therapy from Phillips University, Enid, Oklahoma. Prior to accepting her present position she worked as activity director in nursing homes in Oklahoma and Kansas.

Laufer, 1982, p. 548), or special skills. In service-oriented programs the residents can function as "adopted grandparents" (Greenblatt, 1982, p. 21) by participating with the students in activities which promote on-going relationships.

Nursing homes become involved in intergenerational programs because these programs offer great potential for helping meet therapeutic goals. Capitalizing fully upon this opportunity is more likely if specific goals are defined at the outset. These goals can then direct the structure of the program. If the purpose is to highlight the abilities of oriented residents and encourage reminiscence, the education-oriented programs are quite appropriate. The residents will regain a feeling of usefulness as they pass their knowledge and/or talents on to others. This process of life review will reflect accomplishments rather than failure. Reminiscence can also be utilized as a therapeutic tool in service-oriented programs. As relationships develop, the students will remind the residents of their own childhood experiences. These on-going relationships will become strongly affectionate and almost totally positive for both generations. The residents will have an increased feeling of self-worth as they become engaged in meaningful relationships.

Finding the appropriate teacher is of great importance in setting up an intergenerational program. The compatibility of the teacher and the activity professional will have a major impact on the success of the program. A teacher who recognizes the abilities of older people and feels comfortable in the nursing home setting will set a positive example to the students. If the teacher views the program as beneficial, this will be communicated to the school. The teacher's role as liaison to the school is vital in promoting the long-term continuation of the program.

In the initial stage, the activity professional may need to meet with the principal or school board as well as the teacher. Data about a variety of successful intergenerational programs that have resulted from the cooperative efforts of school systems and nursing homes should be made available to them. A proposal with specific suggestions about the frequency of meetings, number of students and residents to be involved and types of activities should be presented. The school's involvement may not initially fulfill all the nursing home's expectations. However, as the program develops and its benefits become tangible, the school's involvement is likely to increase.

Once the joint proposal has been formed, the activity professional and the teacher can plan specific activities. The objectives of both settings will provide ideas for each session. The oral history class can include discussion topics that center on specific time periods like the Depression or subjects such as early 1900 clothing styles. Trips to museums, old-fashioned picnics, or churning butter can provide actual experiences of history.

In service-oriented programs, relationships between the students and residents will develop as they participate in activities such as designing posters for a health fair, making valentines, or preparing a music performance.

An orientation about the aging process and the nursing home environment will help prepare students for the program. This presentation should include a brief explanation of reasons for nursing home placement and comments regarding rehabilitation, hearing and visual deficits, wheelchairs, canes, restraints, potential resident deaths, incontinency and disorientation. Describing the program's purpose will help clearly establish the students' roles. Students can then be encouraged to ask questions and share their experiences with the elderly and/or nursing homes.

Selection and preparation of the residents must be carefully managed. First, the activity professional must choose which residents are most appropriate for the program. The goals of the program will dictate the criteria for selecting the residents. A program which will require intellectual abilities and group participation is suitable to oriented residents who function well in groups. A program which promotes on-going relationships is appropriate for a long-term resident who consistently attends activities and is able to engage in meaningful communication. Other group dynamics can also play a role in selection. For example, if a husband and wife have a tendency to argue in a group setting, one spouse could be placed in the intergenerational program while the other participates in some other special activity. Interviews of the selected residents can help determine their interest in the program. The residents should be notified of any expectations such as consistent attendance or the sharing of information. If pictures will be taken of the residents or their quotations published, a waiver of confidentiality may be obtained.

Other preparatory steps include determining the location of meetings and staff education. In most long-term care settings, residents' decreased mobility level will necessitate that the activities take place in the nursing home. A room which is well lighted and can be shut off from distractions will be important to the success of the activities. A "Do Not Disturb" sign may be needed to limit interruptions.

Staff education about the structure and benefits of the program will promote their understanding and enjoyment. Furnishing staff members with a schedule and list of residents involved will help them provide baths and medical treatments without interrupting the program. As the program develops, its progress can be shared through memos and/or newsletters.

Intergenerational programs developed with varied grade levels help to satisfy diverse resident and student needs. Having several programs operating with different objectives can increase the number of residents involved. Residents can be assigned to the program which best meets their individual needs and interests. Both small groups and one-to-one sessions can be utilized. An oriented resident who speaks a foreign language can provide one-to-one lessons for a high school student. Third grade students can learn about the adversity, effort and courage of the elderly as they help residents involved in a stroke rehabilitation program. The students will give the residents unqualified and enthusiastic support to recover.

Other aspects of intergenerational programs which may be anticipated are transportation difficulties, resident deaths, and discontinuation of the program during certain periods of time. In many situations, transportation difficulties can be resolved by cooperating with a school that is within walking distance or by utilizing nursing home or school volunteers. Preparation for resident deaths can be handled during the initial orientation. At that time, students can ask questions and express concerns. When a participating resident dies, prompt communication to the teacher and students will allow them to share feelings and work toward acceptance.

For optimum results, the program should be scheduled to follow the entire school year. However, some schools may need to schedule the program only during a certain semester according to the curriculum. A break in the program may also occur during the summer months. After the program has become well established, these gaps may be shortened by enlisting the help of the students' parents. Once the parents become acquainted with the program's benefits, they are likely to advocate its continuation.

Intergenerational programs which utilize the school system have great potential for addressing the diverse needs of nursing home residents. The activity program's resources are expanded by tapping into this rich community resource. The skills of the teacher and the enthusiasm of the students will act as catalysts in promoting residents' involvement. This involvement will allow therapeutic goals to be realized.

REFERENCES

Greenblatt, F. "Adopt-a-grandchild Program: Improving Attitudes of Adolescents Toward the Aged," *Activities, Adaptation and Aging,* 3: 21-25, 1982.

Laufer, E.A., and Laufer, W.S., "From Geriatric Resident to Language Professor: A New Program Using the Talents of the Elderly in a Skilled Nursing Facility," *The Gerontologist,* 22: 548-549, 1982.

Perschbacher, R. "An Application of Reminiscence in an Activity Setting," *The Gerontologist,* in press.

Intergenerational Mixing

Karen D. Schelinder

Each Friday afternoon residents of Tufte Manor Retirement Home assemble in the front lobby of the home and anxiously await the arrival of second grade students from nearby Kelly Elementary School. What happens once the children arrive is the basis for an intergenerational program which is meeting with remarkable success for the residents and their young visitors.

In an article, *Aging Each Other,* Henry M. Plawecki and Judith A. Plawecki state: "Ageism is a convenient mechanism that allows younger people to see older people as different from themselves. Thus, the younger generation subtly ceases to identify with its elders as fellow human beings." Some months ago, to bring about a change in this attitude, the retirement home staff met with the teachers from Kelly Elementary to plan how best to bring together the young and the old.

They discussed a program that would involve 48 second grade students and 25 residents of Tufte Manor. The objective was to assist the residents and children to form new relationships with one another. An hour each week was set aside when the children would walk over to Tufte Manor and spend that time in the environment where older people live. Staff who planned the activity hoped that the younger people would benefit from their contact with older residents in more than one important way. They would make new friends and, equally important, they would spend time in a home where the "old people live" and find it a positive, joyful, exciting place to experience new ideas. This was planned to be a continuing, growing, on-going relationship, not a one-year experience.

The vehicle for interaction is reading. Each child plans for Friday afternoons at Tufte Manor by choosing something to read. The resident might also plan something to read to the children.

Karen D. Schelinder is Housing Manager at Tufte Manor, Grand Forks, North Dakota. She is a graduate of Golden Valley College and a part-time student at the University of North Dakota, Grand Forks. She has completed specialized training in the management of non-profit housing for the elderly.

Once the program was underway, ideas kept coming from other staff members, both at the school and the retirement home. Students saw that the residents were becoming members of an extended family. Parents began coming to visit in the evening with their children, inviting the residents for meals in their homes, and bringing flowers for special days in the residents' lives.

Barriers traditionally known as "generation gap" are coming down. Such effects of integration of the generations as lack of communication, intolerance of handicaps, and stereotypes of aging are disappearing among the participants of this program.

As Carol Tice has stated in her article, *Creating Caring Communities—Linking the Generations,* "Working side by side, old and the young serve as natural teachers to one another." A good example of this is what the children are learning about handicaps and how people cope daily with deficiencies. Before the children started coming to the home, they studied handicaps for one semester. They learned about blindness, wheelchairs, walkers and other aids to mobility. They learned about hearing impairments and how to communicate clearly. They understand that many deaf people read lips. Through this study, they are better equipped to relate to and understand the residents.

Two girls read to a blind lady, Ingeborg. For Ingeborg, Katie and Sarah must explain the pictures on the pages. If they bring drawings for Ingeborg, they also have to explain and describe their art work.

When talking to hearing impaired people, students are learning to speak louder, clearer and sometimes more slowly and to look directly at the person being spoken to.

Close relationships are being built as exemplified by the word *Grandperson,* the students' name for participants in this program. The word *Grandperson* came from the second graders themselves. They coined it after visiting grand people at Tufte Manor. The word "grand" has a very majestic connotation to it; when eight-year-olds think of "grand," they think big and wonderful. Each Tufte Manor resident finds himself in a place of honor, a special Grandperson to a younger individual.

In addition to reading to each other, the participants "tell each other things," in the words of one of the students. The stories they share might include the residents' tales of their growing-up years; the days when they took a horse and buggy to town to buy groceries enough for maybe a month at a time. The young people hear stories about barn dances, other forms of entertainment and how important their churches were to them.

The young people talk about computers, fast fancy cars and how much faster you can move today.

With this experience, it would be hard for a young person to imagine all older people as "lying in bed, waiting to die."

There are several offshoots from the original program idea. The participants have been involved together in woodworking projects, decorating Halloween cookies and sharing meals. At Christmas an afternoon tea was hosted by the residents of Tufte Manor. The second grade students from Kelly School were the special guests. Christmas goodies (all Norwegian delicacies) were served after residents and readers together presented a program that included songs sung by a combined resident/student choir and stories told by the residents. The children's parents and family members of the residents were in the audience.

Informal Friday noon dinners are scheduled each week. Four readers and two residents eat together at the home. This experience provides more personal interaction than the planned 45 minute reading sessions.

A program such as the one described here involves community participation. People in the community learn about needs that are being met by interaction of children and older adults through coverage on television and in the local newspaper. A local television station taped a reading session and aired it with a full explanation of the program's benefits to both young and old. Additional coverage is planned. The local newspaper told about the program with pictures and a warm, personal story about two of the residents and the children who are involved with them.

Parents are a great asset to the success of this program. After the initial planning by school and retirement home staff, parents volunteered to walk the children to and from school. They monitor the halls at Tufte Manor, helping out if a child can't find a room or sometimes needs a little extra security.

It is impossible to record on paper all the rewarding experiences that happen every day between the people involved in this program. The hugs and kisses that are exchanged, the smiling faces and the giggling at a funny story are being shared by the old and young coming together on this one-to-one basis. They are finding the meaning of giving of themselves; they are reaching out and touching in love.

The Day Room Program at Westmoreland Manor Nursing Home, Waukesha, Wisconsin

Jacqueline Brunner

The Day Room Program at Westmoreland Manor was set up in response to a 1981 State of Wisconsin Nursing Home Survey recommendation to increase programming on the 2 North geriatric unit. The initial objectives of the program were to assure that the environment on the unit would increase the mental orientation and physical comfort of the residents there. At the time the day room was opened, the residents on the unit were clearly the most confused, disoriented residents in the nursing home.

STATED OBJECTIVES OF THE DAY ROOM

The objective of the 2 North Day Room program is to assure that the environment is conducive to increasing the mental orientation and physical comfort of the 2 North resident.

Nursing aides will be encouraged to bring their residents to the day room after their morning care has been completed. Once they have been checked in, the day room staff will involve them in appropriate activities, provide mental and physical activity and regularly scheduled outings both in the facility and in the community.

Residents who cannot be managed and are disruptive will be removed from the day room to the nursing station area. Nursing will then determine what action should follow. Under no circumstances

River Hills West in Pewaukee, Wisconsin was extremely helpful in sharing its program and resources. Individuals who contributed much to the success of the program and who merit special recognition are: Gayle Allen-Burket, TRS, Collaboration Consulting Services, Chicago, Illinois; Jean Neitze, RN, Director of Nursing at Westmoreland Manor; Mary Barner, LPN, Day Room Supervisor; and Sherry Lincoln, Day Room Aide.

Jacqueline Brunner is a certified occupational therapy assistant working as an activity director for Westmoreland Manor, Waukesha, Wisconsin.

will the well-being and safety of residents be compromised by a disruptive resident. Such behaviors will be monitored at the nurse's station.

CHECK IN PROCEDURE:

1. Resident is washed and oral care completed.
2. Resident's hair is combed and brushed.
3. Resident is appropriately dressed, including proper and matching socks and shoes/slippers.
4. Resident is wearing glasses, hearing aid and/or dentures if such items are appropriate.
5. Resident has been toileted within one-half hour prior to entering the day room. This time will be reported by aide during check-in procedure.

STATED ROLE OF FLOOR AIDES

Daily care will not really change. Residents will be dressed appropriately and checked into the day room for programs. Residents should be freshly diapered or toileted before checking in. Nursing assistants will be called if a resident requires a major clean up, toileting if diapered or is scheduled for regular bowel and bladder program.

The day room will accept all appropriate residents within the limits of the room and whatever program is running. Some residents will be considered passive participants in the program with the goal of becoming more actively involved. An inappropriate resident is one who is disruptive to other residents and does not respond to positive reinforcement and encouragement. Inappropriate residents will be removed from the day room and checked in with nursing personnel for close monitoring of behaviors.

The luncheon program will only accommodate six residents. They will share a family style lunch with day room staff five days weekly. Reminiscing, manners and conversation will be developed during these luncheons.

Day room staff will work together with general activity staff to continue the large group programs already established on unit. In addition activity staff will work together to improve the environment and living areas for the residents who spend a major part of their day in their rooms and beds.

DAY ROOM SCHEDULE

9:00 to 10:30	Day room supervisor and aide will work on finishing touches of make-up, hair and nail care and oversee the check-in process for day room.
10:30 to 11:30	Day room staff and the activity aide will work together in large group activity.
11:30 to 12:30	Day room personnel will set up for luncheon group, which will include higher level 2 North residents.

Lunch Break for Staff

1:00 to 3:00	Room visits, small group projects in day room. Planning for activities, decorate day room and residents' rooms.
3:00 to 4:30	Large group activity in day room.
4:30 to 5:00	Paperwork as required.

UTILIZATION REVIEW BOARD STUDY

The project served as a Utilization Review Board study from June 1982 through June 1983. During that time we looked at (1) the effect of the day room on residents, (2) the effect of the day room on nursing home administration, and (3) the effect of the day room on families and nursing home placement.

As part of the project a luncheon program was set up to offer as many residents as possible the benefits of family style lunches four times a week. Residents were encouraged to set the table, pass food and serve themselves if possible, to reminisce and converse with peers and staff during the mealtime.

Programming specific to the needs of these residents was developed with the help and cooperation of the Activity Director. The day room staff had the complete cooperation of the general activity staff to continue the large group programs and outings formerly available to the residents on a limited basis. In addition, activity staff and day room personnel worked together to improve the living environment for the residents who spend a major part of their day in the comparatively isolated 2 North area.

EFFECT OF THE DAY ROOM ON RESIDENTS

Although the physical areas for programming were not changed, increased environmental stimulus was added to the room. An indoor garden was planted and kept up, birds in cages were brought in as pets, a dog was added to the unit during the day, and a stereo unit was purchased. The room was transformed into a bright cheery environment by day room staff.

Staff time in activities allotted to the 2 North program prior to November 1981 was approximately 15 hours a week. As of June 1983 staff hours are approximately 70 hours per week.

Prior to November 1981 the residents were offered five specific programs on their unit and allotted two hours weekly for room visits. In June 1983 the residents were offered 30 hours of scheduled programs with five hours for room visits weekly. The day room was staffed from 8:30 to 4:30 p.m. Monday through Thursday and 8:30 to 1:00 p.m. Friday. The schedule was structured to allow programming for activities of daily living, individual crafts and games, and other leisure recreational pursuits appropriate to a geriatric population. An LPN was assigned to be Day Room Supervisor and a nursing assistant as Day Room Aide. Both positions are full time.

As part of the grooming program each morning, approximately three male residents are encouraged to shave themselves. Staff teaches the self help aspect of this grooming skill. Approximately four female residents are taught nail care during this time. Formerly, the nursing staff never had the time for teaching this therapeutic skill.

It quickly became apparent that some residents were responding so well to the increased programming that as they were reviewed at plan of care meetings, a review and frequently a reduction of daily medications was considered. A random sampling of 15 residents shows the following results using a November 1981 base period with review on medications in June 1983: 8 residents decreased in medication, 1 resident increased in medication, 6 residents had no change in medication.

Several residents who lived in the 2 North unit prior to the day room program evidence serious aggressive tendencies which are well documented. The following paragraphs describe five residents who caused major behavioral problems prior to the day room program. The observations in these examples are subjective and given by staff working on the unit with many years of experience.

Resident #1

Formerly yelled, punched and verbally abused anyone for any reason. Never attended activity programs. Was very difficult during activities of daily living. Staff member states, "He is much easier to do activities of daily living now that he is active in the day room."

Resident #2

Known to hit and physically abuse other residents and staff. Was verbally abusive to residents and staff. A program of behavior modification was developed, and the nursing staff and day room personnel have seen a 95% improvement in acting out behaviors.

Resident #3

Was impossible during activities of daily living. Required 2 or even 3 aides to assist. Since day room involvement, needs only 1 aide for ADL.

Resident #4

Very loud disruptive resident, cried much of the time. Is presently much quieter and appropriate when in the day room, although only a passive participant.

Resident #5

Noisy and disruptive before the program and continues these same patterns at present.

In addition to the above, the effect of the day room on residents is evident during a brief walk on the unit. Residents seem more alert, they appear better groomed and happier. They can occasionally be seen interacting with peers and staff on a regular basis. Prior to the day room, some of these observations could be made on isolated cases, but since the day room program began, they are normal everyday occurrences.

EFFECT OF THE DAY ROOM ON NURSING HOME ADMINISTRATION

Although there was some initial resistance to the day room program, staff was counseled and encouraged to cooperate with the program. Over the one and a half years of the program, a marked increase in cooperation and understanding is evident between day room personnel and nursing personnel on the unit.

The Nursing Department has gradually been reducing scheduling on the unit, but with the day room program, quality care for residents is continuing. In the quarter between July 31 through October 22, 1981, nursing assistants were scheduled for an average of 411 hours per weekday shift. In the March 10 through May 19, 1983 quarter, nursing assistants were scheduled for an average of 361.75 hours. This reflects a 48.25 hour weekly decrease in staffing for the unit.

According to figures submitted by the administrator, the 2 North unit averaged 3.5 to 4 empty beds prior to November 1981. Since the program has been in full swing, the unit averages 1 to .5 empty beds.

EFFECT OF THE DAY ROOM ON FAMILIES AND NURSING HOME PLACEMENT

The admissions coordinator notes that she receives placement referrals directly to the 2 North day room unit. Formerly she was unsuccessful in placing new admissions on the unit. The unit was filled by in-house transfers as a resident's needs for a more restricted environment became clear. She also noted that families are requesting the day room program for their family member as a result of their favorable impression of the program during their tour of the facility.

The following observations and comments have been made by family members regarding the day room program.

Family #1

Sister of a resident refused to have the resident in any programs, preferred to have him isolated in his room. She now has given her permission and even comes into the day room to visit briefly with staff.

Family #2

States, "I'm always happy to see Mr. ______ in the day room."

Family #3

Wife wants resident involved in every aspect of program. Was very opposed to resident's transfer from the first floor and had difficulty adjusting to resident's nursing home placement. She now asks, "who has more fun in the day room, staff or residents?"

Family #4

Niece of resident wants aunt involved as much as possible. Has voluntarily asked if resident needed more money to participate in day room outings.

Family #5

Husband of young nursing home resident with complicated physical and emotional problems states, "I'm very glad ______ is active in the day room so she doesn't have to be alone all day." The day room staff is so significant to this resident that the speech therapist has included their names on her very limited communication board.

Family #6

Wife of long time resident states, "I cannot believe the difference in the physical appearance of the residents and the unit," and is amazed in the increase in conversation and socialization between residents.

SUMMARY

The effect of the day room on residents is obvious to any observer. The residents appear to be and are better oriented to their environment. They are busy and happy. There is less crying out and acting out. The unit itself is attractive and stimulating. The residents have a wide variety of programs to choose from and interact daily with peers and staff on an appropriate age level. In some cases decreased medication allows a more normal life. A busier day encourages normal sleep patterns at night.

The effect of the day room on nursing home administration for the unit is one of pride in a job well done. There is an opportunity to view residents as individuals with likes and dislikes. The staff was requested to adjust to a completely new routine for the benefit of residents and has done so. Although nursing aide hours on the unit have been decreased, the day room is staffed using nursing hours, and the unit has worked together to establish a new distribution of work which benefits the residents.

The effect of the day room on families and nursing home placements has been positive. As the report indicates, families are lavish with praise. The reduction of empty beds on the unit is an obvious financial advantage to the nursing home.

REACH

An auxiliary program connected with the day room developed as it became apparent that the 2 North residents needed their rest period during the afternoon and that the Day Room staff was poorly utilized during this period.

The effectiveness and enthusiasm of the Day Room staff also created a strong desire in the general program to open the services of the day room to certain special residents.

The residents viewed with special needs frequently are those newly admitted individuals who are having difficulty adjusting to nursing home placement or those residents whose condition is apparently changing either for the better or worse.

As an answer to the above concerns the REACH program developed. The day room is opened three afternoons each week for specific residents from the other units whose status meets the above criteria. The day room staff provides remotivational and reality oriented programs. They develop purposeful activities to keep residents interested. The staff provides consistency and the group develops peer support and interaction.

As an adjunct to REACH, the day room accepts on a daily basis two severely and profoundly retarded adults from our Developmentally Disabled unit into the regular programming. These visitors benefit from a pleasant change of environment and the tender concern of the day room personnel. Occasionally they are included actively in the program but their passive abilities usually preclude active participation.

Reality Therapy in the Convalescent Home

Sally Vogt

I was a student in Reality Therapy (RT) when I became the Coordinator of Activities at Four Fountains Convalescent Center in Belleville, Illinois. Reality Therapy was developed by Dr. William Glasser, M.D., who has written several books showing the use of it in schools, institutions, and with adolescents, in both groups and in one-to-one personal counseling. Its basis stresses that our behavior—thinking, doing and feeling—is based on our perceptions of the world as we see it.

Reality Therapy allows that we are responsible for our behaviors, and it is this responsibility that can give us control of our own lives. Our thinking, feeling and doing behaviors control our actions and though we are always controlling for our basic needs of food and shelter, we are also controlling for four other needs: belonging, self-esteem, fun and freedom.

I cannot elaborate on all parts of Reality Therapy in this paper. In total, it is concerned with the relationship of the new brain to the old brain: the comparing station in our mind; that our perceptual errors in our comparing station cause us to choose behaviors that may or may not work (such as depressing, paining, headaching); and that we choose these behaviors because they may have worked in the past or we do not know a better way. The point is that by working to meet the needs of belonging, self-esteem, freedom and fun, a person can be happy. Reality Therapy also teaches people to be in process, not outcome. We enjoy our process realizing that the future is out of our control. We stay in today for that is all we have.

The basic four questions that are used in this therapy are:

Sally Vogt is an activity therapist and coordinator of activities at Four Fountains Convalescent Center in Belleville, Illinois. Ms. Vogt earned her AA degree at Monticello College, Godfrey, Illinois, and has received specialized training in reality therapy at the Institute of Reality Therapy in California. She is also a writer and has worked with community advocacy groups for children and youth.

1. What do you want?
2. What do you really want?
3. What are you doing now to get what you want?
4. Is it working?

These basic questions help us to get into another person's world, to see what he wants and also to enable the person to make a value judgment by himself about whether or not his behavior is working. I personally use these questions when visiting with residents instead of the standard "How are . . . " questions referring to how they are feeling, etc.

With this brief background of Reality Therapy, it is also important to know that to teach RT one must incorporate it into his own life. Two inservices were given to the nursing personnel in the Four Fountains Convalescent Center, not only to show how RT can work in our lives, but also how to apply this at work.

Included with Reality Therapy was a background of Independent Living from an Independent Living Organization in St. Louis. Independent Living techniques were taught there to enable a person who was disabled to live independently with dignity. The words "live independently" do not necessarily mean living alone, for that is impossible for some. These words mean to function as an individual with self-esteem and belonging. They refer to the organizing, planning and control of not only the functions of the human body but the use of available resources of the human mind.

In the medical world of hygiene, paperwork, medications and time schedules, there is rarely time to help a resident learn to wheel his own wheelchair, to make decisions of daily living skills and the use of adaptive equipment, to discuss feelings of depression and rebellion, to clarify his confusion with the use of Reality Orientation. This is where the Activity Therapy Department can step in with its program of rehabilitation. This program can truly complement the medical role in a Convalescent Center.

The following is a discussion of how the Reality Therapy techniques are used at Four Fountains.

When a new resident enters the facility, immediate contact is made. A tour of the facility is recommended and includes introducing the activities program, explaining the dining room procedures, etc. The move from a hospital to a convalescent center often is very disorienting. An activity schedule for the week is given to the new resident and an initial care plan devised the first day. This is Reality

Therapy and Reality Orientation working together. In effect I am saying, "This is where you are now; this is what we have. Now, what do you want and what you willing to do to get what you want!" (Of course this does not always work with some residents; but it works for a surprisingly high number of people who respond to and know exactly what I am saying to them.)

To be able to move freely around the facility a non-ambulatory person must learn the mechanics of his wheelchair. Role modeling is a valuable tool for teaching anything. Get in a wheelchair yourself and show the person exactly what you are trying to teach or ask another resident to demonstrate. An added benefit is a very good "eye-to-eye" contact rather than standing over a resident "talking down."

All our activities are taken seriously as Activity Therapy. Our exercises are professionally done by our Physical Therapy Department. There are no spectators during group exercise. All who are in that room, including visitors and personnel, do exercises. Bingo games are an aid to those who are struggling to recognize names and numbers. Word games provide mental stimulation. Music programs reach out to the non-communicative and the disoriented, linen folding provides self-esteem while doing a service type of work. Each activity has a purpose. However, there is much laughter as we share in the joys of small accomplishments.

We use adaptive equipment as much as possible such as jumbo bingo cards for those with limited sight, a portable microphone for those with limited hearing. Radio Information Service for the Blind and large index cards with pertinent words on them for those with limited speech.

Our residents learn that what they can do for themselves they should do; *but* when they cannot do something for themselves, they must learn to ask for help. Asking for help is not easy for a person that has been self-sufficient for 50 years or more. As a matter of example I also have learned to ask for help from the residents in my job.

One of our most successful programs has been our innovative "Rehab Lunch Program." About a third of our residents eat in the dining room. The remaining two-thirds are for the most part disoriented and non-communicative, and completely bedridden. They eat in their rooms or in the day room. Twelve people are selected from the dayroom (3 to a wing) to have lunch with the Activity Therapy Department and the Director of Nurses. We all eat in the Activity

Room. Staff does not assist anyone at this time for this is also *our* lunch period. The trays are served, and we all eat and talk as we would in any other setting. We have discovered an amazing lack of problem eaters with this lunch program. Only an occasional nudge or word of encouragement is needed. Our role-modeling again pays off while teaching people the regaining of lost skills for feeding themselves. Some are "graduated" into the dining room; some go back to the wings with a few added skills.

The problem of offering choices to promote independence and just plain getting a person to come to activities is one that I have heard over and over from other Activity Therapists. As I said before, I use the basic four questions when visiting a resident. A typical conversation is:

> "Good morning. What are you doing?"
> "Nothing" is the inevitable answer.
> "What do you want?"
> "I want to go home."
> "What are you doing to get that?"
> "Just sitting here."
> "Is it helping?" I ask.
> "I don't know" or "What can I do?"
> "How about making a choice today to come to exercises or bingo. It may help you to get what you want, and it is certainly better than sitting here doing nothing."

Doing something is always better than sitting alone depressing and paining. When I cannot reach a person, I leave with the words, "Have a good day. It's your choice, and I'll be back this afternoon to visit." Never give up and never expect unrealistic goals.

As stated before, Reality Therapy teaches that a person will be happy if he is working to meet his own needs. Activity Therapy can be built around these needs of belonging, self-esteem, freedom and fun, allowing a resident to have a choice. Teaching skills to meet these needs is the primary role of a Reality Therapist. Care plans can be worked according to these needs and a resident can take an active part in the skill-building process, learning or relearning how to meet these needs. Activities can be passive or active. We look at the active part of activities as the most important, giving each resident the opportunity to use or learn the necessary skills for his recovery.

REFERENCES

Glasser, William, M.D. *Stations of the Mind.* New York: Harper & Row, 1981.
Glasser, William, M.D. *The Identity Society.* New York: Harper, 1975 (rev.)
Glasser, William, M.D. *Positive Addiction.* New York: Harper, 1976.
Glasser, William, M.D. *Schools Without Failure.* New York: Harper, 1969.
Karrass, Chester L. and William Glasser. *Both-win Management.* New York: Lippincott & Crowell, 1980.

Programming for Optimum Health and Wellness

Mary S. Simper

The main and long term objectives of programming for the aged are: (1) to produce the optimum sense of total wellness possible, and (2) to assist in establishing a positive purpose in life.

Total wellness is the absence of dis-ease. When we are diseased we feel depressed and lethargic, with certain parts of our being stressed. These feelings are reflected in the whole body.

> Everything affects our health, all factors, physical, mental, emotional, spiritual. What holistic health represents is the acceptance of our entire reality: being in our bodies, owning our feelings, attitudes and beliefs, being open to relationships and change and being responsible for every thought, deed and condition we are involved in. (Ryan, 1981)

An aging person can be living to the optimum capacity of wellness even though physically handicapped, in pain, or frail. Whatever our position, there can be an appreciation for ourselves as human beings. We can move toward positive health by accepting situations and finding new meaning to life.

Emotional states of boredom, listlessness, stress, loss of dignity, loss of self esteem and relinquishment of self authority can set the stage for physical dis-ease to manifest through the lowering of the body's resistance. With the reversal of these states comes a sense of well-being. Added positiveness affects the physical being. Symptoms are reversed and further impairments prevented.

Mary Simper is consultant to Bonneville Health Group and plans and assists with programming at an adult day care center and resident home for older women in Salt Lake City, Utah. She holds a BS degree in human relations from Westminster College, Salt Lake City, a graduate certificate in gerontology from the University of Utah, and a PhD in gerontology and holistic health at Union of Experimenting Colleges and Universities, Cincinnati, Ohio.

Dealing with wellness and self-responsibility requires a tuning into oneself and dealing with the whole person. Piero Ferrucci (1982) says:

> The Italian psychiatrist, Robert Assagioli noticed several years ago that a great deal of psychological pain, imbalance and meaninglessness are felt when our diverse inner elements exist unconnected side by side or clash with each other. But he also observed that when they merge in successively greater wholes, we experience a release of energy, a sense of well-being and a greater depth of meaning in our lives.

I find it beneficial to plan programming around the four aspects of the whole person—the physical, mental, emotional and spiritual bodies. Programming involving all four of these areas stands a greater chance of eliciting a response than attention to one or two. When we are locked into one discipline, we are denying ourselves and our clients the benefits of flexibility and creativity. For instance, we ourselves may despise bingo. However, if this is the first activity in which a person will become involved and during that activity he experiences a physical expression of concern, such as a hand held or touch on the shoulder, his participation in other activities may result. If petting a cat or dog, or holding a baby has the same effect, great! Perhaps just sitting quietly listening to music and holding hands will be the beginning.

The following ideas may be helpful in planning holistic programming.

PHYSICAL

1. A suitable routine of physical exercise
2. Discussions on nutrition
3. Relaxation techniques
4. Deep breathing
5. Craft activities
6. Games
7. Recreational activities
8. Discussions on touching, sensuality, sexuality
9. Tai Chi
10. Walking

EMOTIONAL

1. Learning to express oneself assertively
2. Expressing emotions in ways that communicate to others how one is feeling
3. Creating and cultivating close relationships and understanding their importance in later years
4. Discovering one's real needs and finding ways to meet them
5. Learning to make choices (decisions)
6. Realizing that one is *the expert* about oneself
7. Practicing exercises in building self esteem
8. Reminiscing with music and discussion
9. Discussing change, bereavement and death

MENTAL

1. Studying
2. Exploring new areas of interest
3. Learning to appreciate music, art, sculpture
4. Writing poetry
5. Learning to mime
6. Writing a Journal
7. Joining discussion groups on current issues

SPIRITUAL

1. Making decisions about the meaning of one's entire life until the last breath. This concept was suggested by Viktor Frankl fifty years ago in his Logotherapy.
2. Replacing the fears and stresses of aging by love—love of self and love of others. With this realization will come a relaxation and letting go of fear and anxiety and a lessening of physical and mental symptoms.
3. Relinquishing guilt
4. Gaining recognition of the individuality of each being and a connectedness with all things
5. Removing the blocks to one's awareness of love's presence in our lives.
6. Practicing relaxation techniques leading to meditation

To incorporate all these elements into programming involves a long-term commitment. However, I try to make each group setting complete in itself.

I start with the affirmation that each person is his own authority and can participate in each section or not as he desires. I commence with a very simple exercise routine which can be done either sitting or standing. I suggest that each person be responsible for deciding how much to do and when to abstain.

Tai Chi is an excellent form of slow, graceful movement for those who are ambulatory and is also a great form of mental concentration. Certainly music helps during exercise time and just moving as one wills to the music is helpful.

The simple relaxation techniques of deep breathing, tensing and relaxing muscles are helpful in controlling pain and leading to meditative visualization.

Following the exercise routines lively discussion can ensue around the topics of physical touch, sensuality and sexuality. Discussions about extended families can encourage people living in supportive environments to build familial relationships with other residents. Doing very simple personal things for each other, such as polishing fingernails, helping with hair combing can provide opportunities for touching and promote discussions of feelings.

To many older people assertive communication is synonymous with aggressiveness. They need to understand that assertive communication says "I care for me, and I care for you, too. I want to explain how I feel and understand how you feel." Practicing situations and role-playing can be very effective. Helping people understand that everyone has a right to his/her feelings, beliefs and opinions. Developing the ability to communicate these without aggressiveness becomes a great stress reducer and helps to eliminate the feeling of being "victimized."

Forming positive affirmations and using them during relaxation time is a pleasant and effective way to improve one's outlook on life. Making lists of emotions, "good" and "bad," and expressing these feelings allows everyone to share the recognition that others experience emotions and brings about a sense of normality.

Discussion topics that may lead to improved self esteem include:

1. Accept yourself as good.
2. Assume responsibility for your happiness.
3. Assume control over your life.
4. Be sure you always have input regarding things affecting you.

5. Nurture close, loving relationships.
6. Learn that you can be an agent for change.
7. Stand up for yourself.
8. Be in harmony with yourself. True power is not coercive nor demanding nor manipulative.

Memories can be evoked and emotions shared through simple activities rather than in a formal discussion group. Experiences such as making ice cream lead naturally to a sharing of former experiences.

When negative emotions are running high amid residents and staff toward a "difficult" person, starring that person in a combination "This Is Your Life" and "Queen for a Day" can elicit empathy and greater understanding.

A primary concern of older people is memory loss. Open recognition of the fact that we forget all our lives and that the problem only takes on great importance as we age can allay fears and bring forth humorous incidents. Games stimulate memory. Sharing memory aids and methods of orderly planning for bill paying, medical needs, etc. can provide positive support.

Book reviews, especially in resident homes, can become shared experiences with a willing resident preparing a chapter for discussion each time. Books that prove most successful are those that have self contained chapters. Some that have proved successful are *Megatrends* by John Naisbitt, *Love is Letting Go of Fear* by Gerald Jampolski, and *Particular Passions* by Lynn Gilbert and Gaylen Moore.

Journal writing can be a method of positively evaluating a life situation. Individuals who cannot write can be assisted by tape recorders or friends willing to be secretaries.

Discussing and writing different forms of poetry, learning to appreciate music, art, sculpture are other avenues to follow. Personal involvement is always a criterion for enjoyment. Sing-alongs and rhythm bands are successful when the songs are familiar. One does not have to be a musician to lead this type of entertainment. Records and cassettes provide an effective accompaniment, and often a leader will emerge from the group.

Developing the awareness of love's presence in oneself can be an exciting adventure. There is a myth in America that old age is not loveable, that old people are angry and frustrated. I believe that myth can be debunked. People have been taught that love of self is pride and arrogance. They need to learn that only by loving oneself is one able to love others. The sharing of positive loving experiences can help. A "love circle" in which everyone holds hands for a quiet moment of reflection to finish a group session can become a routine closure. During this quiet time names of friends who are absent or sick may be mentioned. Visualizing those friends, or oneself, surrounded by a golden light is a beneficial adjunct. This exercise has been used very successfully when a death has occurred.

A song for closing, with or without movements, can be learned by everyone. The following, taken from a recording, "*On Wings of Song*," (Fretless Records, Philo Records Ferrisburg, VT, 1980) is an example:

> May the blessings of God rest upon you,
> May His peace abide in you:
> May His presence illuminate your heart,
> Now and forever more.

Emphasis on living *now* rather than dwelling on the past can be a positive experience. When circumstances change and anger and frustration result because of an inability to return to past places and lifestyles, it is possible with help to view the situation differently and with more positive feelings. Saint Francis de Sales said:

> "Be patient with everyone, but above all be patient with yourself. I mean, do not be disheartened by your imperfections, but always rise up with fresh courage. I am glad you make a fresh beginning daily. There is no better means of attainment to the spiritual life than by continually beginning again, and never thinking that we have done enough. How are we to be patient in dealing with our neighbor's faults if we are impatient in dealing with our own? He who is fretted by his own failings will not correct them. All profitable correction comes from a calm and peaceful mind."

So exercise, relaxation and deep breathing begin the sessions. Usually a short discussion on some aspect of emotions and dealing with them follows. The "meat" of the group is usually the part dealing with the mental aspect, but flexibility is needed here. Planned activities should be put aside if a need to do something else arises. Closure is always with the "love circle" or quiet time.

Following are some other suggestions to help with programming.

To encourage walking, a mileage chart is effective. Participants select a destination. The area surrounding the home (as well as the hall area which is used in inclement weather) is measured, and the participants record on the chart how far they walk. There can be a celebration as each person reaches his "destination."

Volunteers to help with developing awareness of the arts can be recruited through Arts Councils, Musicians' Unions, colleges and universities, volunteer organizations.

Visiting symphonies, ballets, modern dance, chorus performances can best be experienced by attending dress rehearsals rather than actual performances. This way there is less confusion with wheelchairs and walkers. Dress rehearsals often take place during the daytime and are easier to attend than night rehearsals. Although attendance at functions away from the facility is encouraged, it can be very tiring to physically impaired persons. Sometimes through the same avenues entertainment can be brought to the residence.

REFERENCES

Ferrucci, Pierro. *What We May Be.* Los Angeles: J.P. Tarcher, Inc., 1982.

Frankl, Viktor E. *Man's Search for Meaning.* New York: Pocket Books, Simon and Schuster, 1949.

Progoff, Ira. *At a Journal Workshop.* New York: Dialogue House, 1975.

Ryan, Sara Reginia and Travis W. *Wellness Workbook.* Berkeley, California: Ten Speed Press, 1981.

Innovative "Resident Volunteer" Programming

Dennis Goodwin

One area of programming which provides a double benefit is that of utilizing the volunteer resources of the nursing home community. This turns the tables on the usual concept of "bringing the community into the facility" and allows the residents the opportunity of giving back something to others who have given to them.

There are many creative resident volunteer positions which go far beyond the simple "sock sorting" and "plant watering" type of job. Many individuals require a position they can really "sink their teeth into" in order to feel constructive and rewarded.

Resident volunteer positions can include activities either in or out of the facility. For example, if the resident is able to leave the facility, he could serve as a "host" at a community event such as an art show or give short tours and talks at a local museum.

It is, of course, a shame that the vast amount of knowledge and experience of so many of our nursing home residents often goes untapped. Presenting lectures to Historical Societies or to the Council on Aging would help renew feelings of belonging to the community. One of the best and most formalized techniques of sharing this "historical treasure" is called the Living History Program. In this program, residents utilize a team teaching approach to presenting classes to schools or other organizations. These classes center around particular time periods or historical events.

Another excellent method of including residents in community functions is using their assistance in fundraisers. Ideas for these are nearly unlimited and can include such projects as raising money for a seeing eye dog, for Christmas gifts for needy families, etc. The residents can also contribute their own efforts and talents to the community through such activities as raising plants to give to iso-

---

Dennis Goodwin is an activity program consultant for the Beverly Enterprises nursing homes in Florida. Mr. Goodwin has a BS degree in psychology and six years experience in the recreation field. He is the author of two manuals for activity coordinators.

lated people in the town, repairing "Toys for Tots" toy donations, or making layettes for needy mothers.

There are also many organized volunteer programs in the community which the resident could consider joining. Examples of these would be the Retired Senior Volunteer Program, Foster Grandparents Program, Pink Lady auxiliary in a local hospital, and others.

One of the most enjoyable ways for a group of nursing home residents to volunteer is to give some type of performance. Resident rhythm bands, puppet shows, bell choirs, clown shows, theater groups and skit reading, and resident choruses can provide a lot of "good will" and fun. These do not have to be extremely professional to bring about a warm, enjoyable interaction. Performances such as these would be very welcome at Senior Centers, other nursing homes, or any type of senior citizen organization.

Even if the resident is not able to venture out into the community, his productiveness to his neighbors by no means needs to end. Nearly anything the individual could have done in his earlier home can be done in a nursing home. One of the most innovative ideas is a "Telephone Reassurance Program" from inside the nursing home. It is an easy matter for an Activity or Social Service Director to obtain lists of individuals in the community who are considered "shut-ins." Churches, the Council on Aging, the Sheriff's Department, and other agencies know of such people. Then, depending on the number of interested residents and the time they want to invest, a schedule is set up for calling these individuals on a regular basis, just as in the traditional Telephone Reassurance Program. This would, of course, not only monitor the isolated individual, but supply great social interaction for both participants.

At least one nursing home resident volunteer group sponsored a scholarship for a nurse's aide in order to pay for Licensed Practical Nurse training. This was given as a bonus for excellent work. Fundraising activities could lead to sponsoring a scout troop, adopting a needy family for Christmas, supporting children overseas, and others.

Another method of helping the community which doesn't involve leaving the facility is to sponsor and "staff" a "Mother's Day Out." This could be weekly or monthly, at a set time, and could supply baby sitting to staff members, specific clubs, or to the community in general. In the same vein, the residents could offer to tutor children in such areas as basic reading, writing, or mathematics. This would assist small children who are having some trouble keeping up with their classmates.

Residents who have some ability at craftwork or needlework could give their talents in various ways. Mittens, scarves, or knitted toys would be welcome at Children's Homes. Christmas decorations would be useful if sent to hospitals or similar facilities. In addition to sending the craft items themselves, residents could often sell or raffle the items and donate the proceeds to a worthwhile cause. Sewing skills can also be used to repair torn clothes or sew on buttons for other residents right in the facility.

If the resident wants to turn his volunteerism toward the other residents of his "mini-community," there are unlimited opportunities. One individualized example is called the "Buddy System" in which an alert resident teams up with a somewhat disoriented resident in order to assist him in his daily schedule.

Too often residents who are in the hospital receive no correspondence from those back in the facility. Resident Volunteers can write and send cards, not only to those in the hospital, but to residents who have been discharged or transferred to other facilities. A letter of thanks from a resident would also mean a lot to a volunteer.

When a newly admitted individual enters the nursing home, a resident "Welcome Wagon" goes a long way in easing his adjustment. Two or three residents willing to spend a little time visiting and helping to orient the new person would be extremely helpful, especially to individuals who seem upset about the admission.

Another twist on the babysitting idea is a "Plant Sitting" service for houseplants of employees and volunteers who are going on vacation and are concerned about their living things getting proper care during their absence.

Residents can plan and give parties and celebrations for staff members, volunteers, and family members. They can help celebrate such important events as graduations, promotions, and marriages. Not only can they have parties and social get-togethers for staff and volunteers, but for each other. For example, a "going away party" for a popular resident who is being transferred or discharged, or "Welcome Back" party for a resident returning from a prolonged stay in the hospital would really help support the feeling of "community" within the facility.

These ideas are just a few possibilities for the utilization of Resident Volunteer positions in creating and maintaining more of a feeling of rewarding, self-directed productivity in nursing home environments. In actuality, nearly every volunteer position which can be staffed by a community volunteer can also be staffed by a resident volunteer.

The Good Samaritan Program: Patients as Volunteers

Jan Seville

The quality/quantity issue re volunteers is frequently brought up when Activities Directors meet. Do you have too many or not enough volunteers? Is there an age limit in your volunteer program? What are your volunteers allowed to do? Sometimes we, as Activities Directors, may not look closely enough at what resources we have at hand . . . our own patients. What more readily available volunteer could we ask?

Several years ago I started an in-house volunteer program at the facility where I work. I chose the name "The Good Samaritans" for the volunteers—our very own patients.

The program contributes to the mental, emotional and social well-being of our patients within the institution. Involvement in such a program can give new meaning to a patient's life. We attempted to build on existing strengths and capabilities, and establish feelings of pride and personal worth as a result. Volunteers can receive pleasure and self-satisfaction from their involvement and at the same time expand their personal interests.

The philosophy of the Good Samaritan Program reflects the general purpose of the activities program as a whole—promoting "meaningful activity." As it is further stated in the code of the New York State Health Department these purposeful activities should "promote and maintain a sense of usefulness to self and others."[2]

This special volunteer program must also follow certain principles. The program must meet the needs of the institution, relating to the objectives of the Activities department. The needs, interests

Jan Seville is activities director at LeRoy Village Green Nursing Home and Rehabilitation Center, Inc., LeRoy, New York. Ms. Seville holds a BS degree in "Community and Human Services with Special Emphasis in Therapeutic Recreation with the Elderly and Handicapped" and is registered as a Therapeutic Recreation Specialist with the National Therapeutic Recreation Society.

[2]New York State Department of Health. Code for Skilled Nursing Facility. 731.6(1)(iv), 1978, 5723H.

and abilities of each patient must be considered. Caution must be taken not to violate the rules and regulations of the state code. Under the patient's and resident's rights, number 10 ensures that each patient/resident "is not required to perform services for the facility that are not included for therapeutic purposes in his plan of care."[3]

Once a patient is accepted into the Good Samaritan Program, his or her involvement must be incorporated into the individual care plan. Each person's projects or duties are presented at care conferences and documented in quarterly reviews. Goals formulated through this program for "therapeutic purposes" are also charted.

Within the first 48 hours of an admission, we, as Activities professionals, begin to learn about our new patient—his/her limitations, abilities and interests. As this patient adjusts, whether he or she becomes involved in activities groups or stays aloof, talents, desires, or needs relevant to the program may be discovered in the individual. That person is then approached to join the Good Samaritan Program.

Posters recruiting Good Samaritans, an article in the facility's newsletter, or an announcement made at Residents' Council meeting have all been effective in increasing the number of volunteers. Word of mouth and peer influence have also contributed to increased membership.

Like other prospective volunteers, those interested fill out applications. Written applications, I feel, serve several purposes. First, they are an official sign-up for the patients. The information obtained is documented feedback of the patients' interests and schedule preference. Then, too, the application denotes membership for the patient.

The format of the application can vary but should include certain necessary information. Useful data include: name; room number; date signed up; time of day preferred (morning, afternoon, evening—weekday, weekend); interests (with a checklist of areas in which volunteers are needed, plus a line for their suggestions).

The second part of the application is for "office use only." In this latter part staff makes an initial charting of projects in which the Good Samaritan is involved. This is convenient for a comparison of the assignment with what the volunteer initially requested. The concluding part for office use is used to log the dates on which the Good

---

[3]New York State Department of Health. Code for Skilled Nursing Facility. 730.17(10), 1980, 5712H and Residential Health Care Facility. 414.14(10), 1980, 4615H.

Samaritan was honored for services and the type of awards presented.

A resident's individual qualifications are not judged as critically for this program as are the community volunteers'. A confused or agitated person can function with simple tasks, although a minimal ability to follow directions is helpful. A stroke victim may need adapted techniques or equipment, but can still offer his or her services.

Of course, time and willingness help, even though the volunteer might prefer a certain day or time. Sincere interest sparks enthusiasm and that in turn encourages responsibility and dependability. Often, because the project is governed by specific needs or requirements, the volunteer must also be willing to take directions.

Organization of the program takes very little work or preparation, especially when compared with the community volunteer program. Once the needs of the program are established, related projects are set up accordingly. As soon as response from an applicant is received, the volunteer can be assigned a specific project according to his or her needs, interests, goals and abilities.

The goals of this Good Samaritan In-House Volunteer Program are subdivided into two areas. The first is related to the goals of the Activities department, and the second is related to the individual volunteer. Outstanding goals may include, but not be limited to, making life more meaningful for the individual, preserving the individual's dignity, promoting the patient's well-being, and providing for the constructive use of leisure time.

This volunteer program should, whenever applicable, try to help each individual Good Samaritan meet his/her own goals. Assistance can be given by assigning related projects to the individual, thus creating opportunities for goals to be reached.

Goals may be short-term (or immediate) and long-term. They include fun and personal enjoyment as well as a sense of achievement. Other appropriate goals are an increase in self-confidence, promotion of self-worth or feelings of usefulness, and the continuation of work interests through work substitute projects. A sense of identity may be maintained, and attitudes toward self and others enriched.

Fun and personal enjoyment can result for patients simply from being out of their rooms, enjoying what they are doing. Perhaps, if several are working on projects together (be it the same or a different project), they enjoy being with others and socializing while they work.

The Good Samaritan Program can serve as a means to increase self-confidence and self-worth. Both are received when a resident shares a musical, craft or cultural talent; they receive praise from peers for a job well done. The responsibility of raising and lowering the American flag is considered a special honor by a legally blind resident of ours, a retired policeman. A former pianist for the silent movies now enjoys playing for our parties. A former secretary types our internal newsletter.

Attitudes toward others can be enriched when people do "favors" for others. Good feelings are a two-way street. Patients learn to feel good about departments within the institution and the departments gain added respect for the patients. When patients can assist a department through a specific task (which is also beneficial for them), positive attitudes are increased. Several examples of these tasks are making tags for laundry, wrapping plasticware in napkins for picnics by dietary and making door decorations for the Activities department. When a patient is assigned to visit other patients or to write letters for them, new friendships can develop.

The Good Samaritan Program helps to meet all these goals and needs through its various projects. Listed below are many of the projects from which our department, facility and patients benefit.

—deliver newspapers
—raise and lower flag
—read to patients
—telephone assurance calls to elderly alone in community
—type (internal newspaper, large print songsheets)
—make laundry tags
—bring out/take in patio furniture cushions
—wrap plasticware for picnics
—friendly visits with patients
—write letters for patients
—share musical talent (i.e., piano at parties)
—teach craft or prepare craft supplies for "kits"
—propel wheelchairs to/from activities
—make place tags or decorations
—pass napkins at parties
—pass bingo cards, chips, prizes, assist others

The Activities staff always works to stimulate the Good Samaritan volunteers, keeping them enthusiastic and motivated. A sincere thank-you is voiced upon completion of each task, no matter how small. A written thank-you note for doing an unusual or larger, more involved project is visible and more lasting than a verbal acknowledgement. Periodically, about every six months, the Good Samaritans are honored formally for their services.

Initially I chose this frequency for three reasons: (1) The health conditions of our Good Samaritans were susceptible to change which might necessitate dropping out of the program. (2) With new admissions to the facility, new possibilities for the program are allocated, and (3) With limited opportunities for gratification of needs within the institution, more frequent formal recognition seemed desirable. The first reason has not proved relevant; however, (2) and especially (3) are quite valid.

To enhance your special luncheons for your Good Samaritans, consider these following suggestions:

1. Deliver formal invitations the day before.
2. Invite department heads who are able to attend.
3. Use china and silver services, especially if different than the dietary's everyday kind.
4. Have your Good Samaritans help prepare part or all of the meal.
5. Music can enhance this special occasion.
6. Give a small speech to your guests regarding the value of their work to your department and the facility.
7. Present certificates of appreciation, encouraging applause after each for immediate individual acknowledgement as their name and duties are announced. An official handshake at this time binds the sincerity of appreciation.
8. Take their pictures with award to mount in the hall for public awareness within the facility. These pictures can later be theirs for a souvenir of the occasion.
9. Have your local newspaper cover this event and thus increase the outside community's awareness.

We have found a multitude of values in our Good Samaritan Program. The values are subdivided into three major categories: social, psychological and personal. Resulting under the social values are a concern for the well-being of others and social interaction. Cooperation is also encouraged. The program creates a better morale between patients and departments, thus promoting unity within the institution.

The psychological benefits include non-monetary rewards, received through promoting a sense of usefulness. The need for recognition is fulfilled. Both rewards and recognition can be verbal, as in a thank-you, or material, as in a certificate, pin or a paragraph written in a newsletter.

Personal values may be continued through pursuing work-type interests or work substitute projects, thus giving the feeling of productivity. The program may contribute to a sense of identity. Personal worth is enhanced through accomplishments which promote dignity.

Sometimes people do not expect help from the underdog. Like the original Good Samaritan in the Gospel of Luke, who was not expected to help the person who was mugged, our patients are not normally considered by non-professionals to be able to help or do anything. But they are—they can—and they do!!

In conclusion, the Good Samaritan In-House Volunteer Program is an extremely useful and rewarding program to the patients, as well as to the Activities department and institution as a whole. All projects within the program, no matter what type, contribute to the patient's constructive use of leisure. The program is an outlet for creativity, sharing and caring.

Patients are encouraged to use their talents and abilities to their fullest. Through promoting feelings of usefulness, self-esteem is increased. Self-esteem enhances self-confidence; both create a positive self-image.

The Good Samaritan Program can be an Activities department's right hand. I return to the issue of quality/quantity frequently brought up in reference to volunteer programs. With our immediate resource of patients/residents, we have quantity from which to choose and use according to our need. And with patients/residents who want to be involved, we have quality because they find reward in being useful.

Veteranship for Nursing Home Residents: Integrating Residents Into Volunteer Services

Lyndon S. Drew

Nursing home residents can contribute their time and talents to community projects. This paper highlights programs which offer residents the opportunity to volunteer. We conclude with a comprehensive description of the Handi Group sponsored by the United Way Retired Senior Volunteer Program (RSVP) of Wichita, Kansas.

Older Americans are making substantial investments in community life. Communities have tapped their resources through the ACTION volunteer programs of RSVP, Foster Grandparents, and Senior Companions. Marjorie Janz recently summarized the benefits of RSVP this way: "The activities of RSVP are meaningful to the old volunteer precisely because they address genuine areas of need in the community" (Janz, 1981, p. 261).

Communities have been slow to recognize nursing home residents as a resource. Friedman, writing in 1975 about volunteer services in one home, observed, "Those who are institutionalized have been neglected in the belief that they themselves are too impaired both mentally and physically to be suited for such involvement" (Friedman, 1975, p. 362). The programs described below belie the belief that residents cannot be involved in volunteer services.

Two important theoretical justifications for service equally apply to older Americans regardless of their residence. Anthropologists have found reciprocity an important social norm in all ages. In a study of residents in public housing projects for the elderly in Mil-

---

Lyndon S. Drew is assistant professor and field placement supervisor of the Gerontology Center at Wichita State University, Wichita, Kansas. With BA, MA, and PhD degrees in political science, he combines an interest in public policy and gerontology.

waukee, Jonas and Wellin found, "The givers have opportunities to play useful and needed roles, in return for rewards ranging from socio-emotional gratification and heightened self-esteem to material compensation" (Jonas and Wellin, 1980, p. 237). Another anthropologist, Gloria Wentowski (1981, p. 608), concluded, based on a study of reciprocity, that "the need to contribute" was "essential to people of all ages."

A second theoretical perspective is offered by Douglas Nelson, who argues that the idea of veteranship could liberate "productively the energy, creativity, and experience of the old" (Nelson, 1982a, p. 166; 1982b). Veteranship understands old age as a measure of experience. The idea, according to Nelson, implies that public policy should promote "programs that utilize the life experience skills of older persons" (Nelson, 1982a, p. 161). Volunteer services recognize the veteranship of older Americans.

This paper proposes to demonstrate that nursing home residents are veterans with skills to share and that nursing home residents, like other older Americans, find meaning in useful lives.

RESIDENT VOLUNTEERS

Residents at Miller's Merry Manor, Inc. of LaGrange, Indiana, are finding the mutual benefits of intergenerational programming (Warner, 1981). The residents began in 1980 to help students with their studies at the Parkside Elementary School in LaGrange. The project's success encouraged Clay School, a school for the developmentally disabled, and the local junior high and nursery schools to request volunteers.

The literature on intergenerational programming documents its value both to the young and to the old (Parnell, 1980). For example, the Teaching-Learning Communities project in Ann Arbor, Michigan, is credited by the director of the Ann Bach Nursing Home with saving "the lives of some of our seniors who were literally giving up their spirit" (Doyle, 1976, p. 30). The residents benefited because they were sharing their lifetime accumulation of skills with the children in the Ann Arbor public schools.

Residents of Briarfield, Inc. in Sylvania, Ohio are helping severely and profoundly retarded children who live in Sunshine Children's Home (Pitzen, 1983). The residents had volunteered within the nursing home by assisting with the care of fellow residents. The

Sunshine program gave them an opportunity to work outside the home.

The staff trained the volunteers with slide presentations on mental retardation and the Sunshine Home. During a tour of the Sunshine Home, staff and volunteers discussed the children's and the volunteers' needs. Recruits were then paired with children. Since October 1, 1981, 22 volunteers, a quarter confined to wheelchairs, have worked alternate Thursdays with the retarded children. Volunteers have found "a new purpose for living" (Pitzen, 1983, p. 37).

The Retired Senior Volunteer Program has enlisted 300 nursing home residents in Montgomery County, Maryland. All of these volunteers help other residents within the homes as did the Briarfield residents; but, 18 residents are helping in the community, in schools, day care centers, public libraries, and other non-profit agencies ("Nursing Home Residents," 1981).

About 125 residents help the community without leaving their homes. These residents are making flash cards and picture books for hospitals and schools and recording books for blind children. Other activities include mailings for the American Heart Association and telephone reassurance for people living alone in the community ("Nursing Home Residents," 1981). The residents who cannot get out freely are making a contribution in Montgomery County, Maryland (National Citizens' Coalition for Nursing Home Reform, 1981).

Fifty residents of nursing homes in Gainesville, Florida, have joined RSVP and assumed the role of service provider ("RSVP Brings Volunteering," 1982). Again, these residents did not need to leave their homes. Like the 300 residents in Maryland, Gainesville volunteers are helping in the care of their fellow residents. Some volunteers are matched with other residents who need help with eating. Some volunteers deliver mail within the home. Like the 125 residents in Maryland, Gainesville volunteers are also helping with community projects. They have prepared large mailings for community organizations. The result is a new role as a caregiver.

All of these cases illustrate the veteranship and generosity of nursing home residents. They have skills and experience to share and they derive meaning from a life of service. Some programs begin with apprehension and uncertainty. Can a nursing home resident help a student? Some programs find opportunities within the home as well as in the community. Some of the volunteers help other residents of the home; some help residents of the community. The potential of residents as volunteers has been demonstrated but not replicated in many homes. To facilitate replication, this paper now draws on the experiences of a previously undocumented RSVP project.

RSVP OF WICHITA, KANSAS

RSVP of Wichita, Kansas, recognized in 1982 that many residents of Wichita's nursing homes could contribute to community projects. Given a choice, residents might welcome the opportunity to work in the community.

In September, 1982, Alexine Larson, a volunteer, began the Handi Group with residents meeting twice a month at Immanuel Lutheran Church. Within a year, the volunteer group grew to a size of 25 to 30 residents and moved to the new downtown senior center. Five homes, Catholic Center for the Aging, Christ Villa, Hillhaven, Lakewood, and Wichita Care Center participate in the program.

The work projects include clerical work for community non-profit organizations such as United Way, March of Dimes, American Cancer Society, the Wichita area office of the state Department of Social and Rehabilitation Services, and the Child Care Association. A typical task is the preparation of newsletters or brochures. The Handi Group also assembled 10,000 pins for United Way's annual fundraiser.

The key to the success of the group is the volunteer coordinator. Alexine Larson invests a week in the execution of each month's work. The volunteers work on a Friday from 9:00 a.m. to 2:30 p.m. Larson begins the Monday before by calling each participating home to find out that week's roster of participants. Then she can call the Metropolitan Transit Authority to arrange for transportation.

Transportation has been a continuing problem. The nursing homes have not been willing or able to use their own vans to transport residents. RSVP now spends $67 a week for specialized transportation services. The cost of transportation forced RSVP to cut back work days for the group from two to one each month.

A second day would now require another volunteer coordinator because of the time commitment. The physically and sometimes mentally impaired volunteers take a lot of supervision. Even with two volunteer assistants, the coordinator is busy.

The coordinator must make final arrangements on Thursday, the day before the Friday work day, for transportation and meals. At first, the meals-on-wheels program served the Handi Group, but the meals were not much different from the meals in the nursing homes. RSVP then tried snack packs from Kentucky Fried Chicken. These meals were so popular that RSVP decided to use them in addition to the food service offered at the downtown senior center. This adds variety to the menu provided to the volunteers.

Not all residents are capable of participating in Handi Group. Each volunteer must fill out the standard volunteer registration form. The work is assigned according to the volunteers' capabilities. Some can staple; others can collate. They all need recognition and encouragement as they complete their work assignments. For these volunteers, the work is a godsend. The work is meaningful and offers volunteers an opportunity to leave the nursing home environment. The volunteers find usefulness and friendship. Many volunteers meet old friends from nursing homes where they previously lived. Only one volunteer has ever complained that the experience was disagreeable. The group of volunteers finds the monthly meeting a real joy.

Community organizations have welcomed the participation of the Handi Group. A staff member of RSVP, Phyllis Bauman, arranges the work on Monday or Tuesday in time to pick it up on Thursday from the agency for Friday's work day. The project is returned as quickly as possible. The agencies have been a satisfied partner.

RSVP budgets $50 a month for meals and $67 a month for transportation. Staff time is necessary to arrange the work. Volunteer time is necessary for coordination and supervision. The activities directors must see that the residents are ready to be picked up on Fridays. This investment in time and money is minimal compared to the opportunity given the volunteers.

HOMEBOUND

Residents of two nursing homes, Green Meadows Nursing Center and Homestead Health Center, have participated in the RSVP homebound program. Residents of Homestead Health Center volunteered for the Handi Group for three months but switched to the homebound program from 9:15 a.m. to 12:30 p.m. on the first Tuesday of each month. Residents of Green Meadows Nursing Center devote each Thursday morning to homebound projects.

RSVP of Wichita is enlisting many homebound persons, in private homes as well as nursing homes, to work on community projects. Work is arranged by the RSVP office personnel as it is for the Handi Group. The difference is the work site.

The work is important to the volunteers because it is for someone else's benefit. As one volunteer said, "I just like to help others. I can't get out anymore, and this is one way I can do that" ("Seniors Lend Helping Hand," 1983).

Participation is limited to the twelve Green Meadows and eight Homestead residents who volunteer. Still, the participation is important. Two women who did not do anything else at Homestead Health Center volunteered for RSVP. One deaf woman who only watched television before her participation in RSVP began to make a few crafts after her participation in RSVP. Two people who were too fearful to leave their room began to participate in RSVP within the home.

As a front page article in a suburban daily reported, the volunteers have stuffed "pledge envelopes for the Labor Day Jerry Lewis MD Telethon, . . . made picture scrap books from greeting cards for Head Start preschoolers, sized and folded T-shirts for the Epilepsy Foundation, made braided jump ropes from bread wrappers for the Institute of Logopedics, and made soft fabric therapy balls for Starky Developmental Center" for mentally retarded children ("Seniors Lend Helping Hand," 1983). These are all meaningful projects benefitting community agencies and their clients and filling what otherwise might have been aimless days. The nursing home and RSVP staff and volunteers agree that the Handi Group experience is superior to the homebound experience. The problems are coordination and transportation. Where time and money are unavailable, the homebound alternative offers more residents the opportunity to volunteer.

VETERANSHIP

The RSVP Handi Group and homebound program demonstrate that nursing home residents have a contribution to make to the community. The concept of veteranship offers activity personnel and volunteer coordinators, a sophisticated rationale for the development of more opportunities for service across the country.

This paper has attempted to give the essential details of the existing program so that developers can replicate and embellish current experience. A sophsticated rationale should not obfuscate the simplicity of the idea. Phyllis Bauman explained it well. "We tend to put older people on the shelf and say they're not worth anything. This gives them meaningful work, really helping someone" ("Seniors Lend Helping Hand," 1983). To people who think of nursing homes as warehouses for the dying, the idea of veteranship for residents will seem absurd, even dangerous. Nursing Home residents need not fear the poor farms of yesteryear or the mental institutions of yesterday when work was a coercive penalty or a corrective therapy. The essence of veteranship is choice. Residents entering a nursing home today need not leave their neighbors behind. Inside or outside the home, resident volunteers can lend their neighbors a helping hand.

REFERENCES

Doyle, J.R. "Digging for Human Treasure." *Educational Leadership,* 34: 26-30, 1976.

Friedman, S. "The Resident Welcoming Committee: Institutionalized Elderly in Volunteer Services to Their Peers," *The Gerontologist,* 15: 362-367, 1975.

Janz, M. "RSVP and a Meaningful Later Life," In F. J. Berghorn, D.E. Schafer & Associates, *The Dynamics of Aging,* Westview, Boulder, Colo., 261-264, 1981.

Jonas, K. & Wellin, E. "Dependency and Reciprocity: Home Health Aid in an Elderly Population," In C.L. Fry (Ed.), *Aging in Culture and Society,* Brooklyn: J.F. Bergin, 1980.

National Citizens' Coalition for Nursing Home Reform, *A Guide to Developing Retired Senior Volunteer Programs Nursing Home Projects,* Program Assistance Paper #16. Washington, D.C.: ACTION, Older American Volunteer Programs, February, 1981.

Nelson, D. "Alternative Images of Old Age as the Bases for Policy," In B.L. Neugarten (Ed.), *Age or Need? Public Policies for Older People,* Beverly Hills: Sage, 131-169, 1982a.

Nelson, D.W. "The Meanings of Old Age for Public Policy," *National Forum,* Fall, 1982b: 27-30.

"Nursing Home Residents Join RSVP," *Aging,* January-February 1981: 35-37.

Parnell, K. "Young and Old Together: A Literature Review," *Childhood Education,* January: 184-188, 1980.

Pitzen, S. "Residents Volunteer for Sunshine," *Nursing Homes,* May/June 1983: 36-37.

"RSVP Brings Volunteering to Nursing Homes," *Aging,* January-February 1982: 32-33.

"Seniors Lend Helping Hand Through RSVP Program," *The Daily Reporter,* September 12, 1983. p. 1.

Warner, J.A. "Aging Residents Become School Volunteers," *Nursing Homes,* July/August 1981: 20-23.

Wentowski, G. "Reciprocity and the Coping Strategies of Older People: Cultural Dimensions of Network Building," *The Gerontologist,* 21: 600-609, 1981.

The Activity Coordinator as Environmental Press

Edward F. Ansello

To many people the term "environmental press" suggests pressure. In fact, environmental press does not necessarily have anything to do with pressure.

In philosophy we learn about the concept of the "Me" and the "Not Me." Environmental press is the "Not Me" for everyone. Each of us is a part of the other's environmental press. The term environmental press includes all the elements around an individual that have an impact or an effect upon that individual. With the definition in mind, you can see that we are part of the environmental press of the residents in the facilities where we work.

ACTIVITIES AND LIFE SATISFACTION

Let us examine the interplay of activities and life satisfaction and the critical role of the activities coordinator in the life satisfaction of residents in long term care. We will discuss the following:

1. The factors in life satisfaction.
2. The importance of activities in life satisfaction. You will see that they have a significant role to play.
3. The importance of your own education to the well-being of the residents.
4. The Environmental Press Model as a way of understanding how you and your residents interact for mutual betterment.
5. Finally, some examples of creative environmental press.

Edward F. Ansello, PhD, is associate director of the Center on Aging of the University of Maryland, College Park. He is the founder of the Maryland Consortium for Gerontology in Higher Education, Inc., a group of institutions working for the advancement of aging-related education, research, and training.

1. Factors in Life Satisfaction

For some time, I have been researching the contributing factors in life satisfaction for those who are institutionalized and also life satisfaction for retirees. Surprisingly, the factors seem to be the same for both groups.

I have organized the findings of this research from most central to the less central contributors. To illustrate their relationship, we can imagine a sphere. The core of this sphere we will label the primary factor in life satisfaction for our groups. The No. 1 factor is the presence or absence of an intimate interpersonal relationship, i.e., someone in whom you can confide, someone who will accept you, maybe get angry but will still be there when the dust settles. The relationship need not necessarily be sexual or marital, but it must be someone who cares and who is cared for in return. Most men identify their wives as their intimate interpersonal confidante. Women, on the other hand, do not necessarily identify their husbands as such, partly because women in late life have outlived their mates. Even for women still married, however, a girl friend is as likely as the husband to be identified as the confidante. This may, of course, reflect female socialization.

Surrounding the core of the sphere is the No. 2 factor in life satisfaction. This outer layer we can call social interpersonal relationships, i.e., friends of substance, people with whom you share time and share interests and similar backgrounds. Men claim to have more friends generally, but they share less information with them. Women claim fewer close friends but their friendships have greater depth.

The No. 3 factor in life satisfaction is activities. In our illustration I would like you to think of an arrow shooting through the sphere, permeating the first two factors. It may even be the factor that holds No. 1 and No. 2 together. Meaningful activities may be the "stuff" of intimate and social interpersonal relationships. Significantly the activities may also exist without them.

The No. 4 factor is money.

Please note that health is not included in these top factors contributing to life satisfaction. A growing body of research suggests strongly that self-perceived health may be a more important factor than clinically measured health as a predictor of how long and how well a person will live. If you have factors 1, 2, and 3, you are likely to perceive your health as good, even if you have debilitating conditions. And so, health here may be a reflection of these more primary factors.

2. *The Importance of Activities in Life Satisfaction*

Now keep in mind the three factors of life satisfaction we have talked about and consider the status of the typical nursing home resident in the life care facility. A female, she is probably there because she has outlived her husband. In 20% of the cases, she has outlived her eldest male child. The No. 1 factor, the intimate interpersonal relationship, has been severed.

Factor No. 2, friends of substance, have been reduced in number because of death, moving or because the resident is in your facility. The friends are not there or cannot be there as often as they would like. There are many people around, but it is artificial to assume that residents thrown together in an institution are going to bond in the same way as those who have shared thirty or forty years together in a community.

So, factor No. 3 is the only meaningful factor in life satisfaction that remains from the top three. From that you can see the activity professionals are profoundly important in life satisfaction. You are central to the life satisfaction, to the very living of the residents in your facility.

3. *Education for the Activity Professional*

Activity coordinators need to know how crucial they are and how to educate themselves. Let's look at five reasons why activity professionals need education.

1. Education comes from the Latin word *educare* meaning "to draw out of." We have skills and abilities in ourselves. Education draws on that which is inside of us. The early concept of education was that it is a one-time inoculation against ignorance. Once a person was done with school, he need never study again. You sometimes hear this translated into the work situation when a supervisor says, "A person should have the skills I'm looking for before I hire him." Such a person disparages education. He assumes that you are everything you are going to be before you take the job. Or a person who does not value education will say, "I did go to a continuing education class in 1981. I'm done for the '80s."

You have undoubtedly heard the saying that a little knowledge is a dangerous thing. It is very easy to become complacent when we have a little information or education under our belt. But we will see that the more we do the same things the less stimulating we become.

2. As an illustration of my second reason for needing education, consider convoys in World War II. The basic principle was that the convoy could go no faster than its slowest ship. Consider services to the aging as a convoy. I know that you do not want the activity professionals to be the slowest ship, retarding the growth of services to elders or of the aging movement.

3. Misconceptions not displaced by factual education can lead to harmful and wasteful consequences in materials and human lives. Let us look at one example of that statement. Today almost half of all 127 medical schools in the United States offer their students some practicum, course, or experience in geriatrics. Yet, in 1982 only 2% of the graduating class had taken advantage of that geriatric experience—and that represented the highest percentage ever!

The results of this lack of education are unfortunate and predictable. The Administration on Aging recognizes a tremendous amount of over-institutionalization. Physicians or family members put residents in institutions because physicians do not have adequate knowledge of alternatives, networks, and available resources.

4. The zeal that a lot of us bring to direct services cannot continue indefinitely; it needs to be reinforced and complemented by knowledge of administrative programming, resources management, and other management skills on the one hand and interpersonal skills and service community skills on the other hand.

5. Our clientele requires us to grow. If you look at a birth cohort, people born at the same period of time, you will see that as age increases, members of the cohort become more diverse, less and less like each other. The least alike people we could ever work with are older people. Our experiences and observations tell us that; research has confirmed it. So we need to *learn* variety, elaborations, creative content and approaches.

Our education can come from a variety of sources. It need not be formal course work. Museums, for example, are offering excellent educational materials. One such traveling exhibit that visited many cities last year is entitled "What About Aging—Your Changing Senses." It is a combination of exhibits, seminars, first-hand experience, tests, and self-assessment to help people learn more about aging.

In Indianapolis, Indiana, Purdue University and the Indiana University have combined efforts and are offering short-term seminars, day-long programs, and community workshops in shopping centers and department stores. The program is entitled "Shop and Learn." Some 15,000 people have taken advantage of a program that offers convenient continuing education.

You have a role in shaping your education. Community colleges are beginning to turn to local Area Agencies on Aging to obtain descriptions of the skills needed to perform jobs related to the elderly. This information is translated to the curriculum. Activity professionals need to feed information to community colleges and local schools so that eventually we will have competency-based education for this profession.

4. The Environmental Press Model

Competence relates to life satisfaction. People who feel competent feel satisfied with life. You recognize this fact as it relates to your job. You are unhappy when you feel overwhelmed or underwhelmed.

M. Powell Lawton has examined the relationship between competence, environment, and adaptation. His Environmental Press Model is simplicity itself.

Visualize a graph on which the vertical axis represents "competence" and the horizontal axis represents "environmental press." From the point where the two lines meet competence progresses upward from low to high. Environmental press increases from weak at the left to strong at the right.

Competence has been found in research literature to be made up of four types: (1) biological or health, such things as mobility, continence, ability to lift a certain weight, ability to bend over, etc.; (2) sensori-motor, how our senses take in information and our bodies react accordingly; (3) cognitive, intellectual skills, or mental ability, and (4) emotional, our stability or ego strength. Each of us has different levels of competence. For our purposes here we will discuss competence in the aggregate or general competence.

Environmental press can be measured and quantified in different ways, according to research at the Philadelphia Geriatric Center and elsewhere. These include:

(1) Segregate Dimension, the degree of segregation among resi-

dents and staff. Are the confused in one room, the non-confused in another? Is there real separation between staff and administration? Is there a sense of ''us'' versus ''them?''

(2) Congregate Dimension, the degree of individual versus categorical application of the rules. Suppose a man who does not leave his room asks for a book to read. If concern for the congregate is stronger than for the individual, he may be told ''Well, the book cart will be coming around next Thursday.'' Is there an individual or group quality to activities?

(3) Related to these dimensions is that of institutional control, the emphasis upon staff versus resident control over behavior. Sometimes dependency factors are built into the institution. Some staff will say that the facility operates best if residents rely on them.

(4) Structure Dimension, the tolerance or intolerance of ambiguity. This dimension concerns the emphasis upon order versus tolerance of some disorder.

(5) Stimulation Dimension, the simplicity or complexity of the opportunities or the activities offered. How rich is the sensory and social environment? Are there only three or four kinds of activities offered? Are they offered with insufferable regularity? A rich environment will include social and intellectual activities, sensorimotor and emotional activities.

(6) Affect Dimension. The environment can either encourage or discourage affectual (or emotional) expression among residents. Years ago staff used to separate residents who they felt were getting too friendly.

(7) Impulse Control. To what extent does the environment offer immediate versus delayed gratification of needs? Can a person have tea or a snack, for instance, at 3:00 in the morning?

All of these dimensions and others can be reduced to three: how much stimulation, change, and responsibility does the environment allow?

The Model

The environmental press model says, in essence, that adaptation to an environment, whether it is the office, marriage, or the long term care facility, is the interaction of the individual's competence and the environment's press.

Looking at our illustration of the Environmental Press Model, we see a linear relationship. If one dimension—competence—goes up, the other dimension—environmental press—should go up for the individual to remain adapted. If you have very low competence, you need weak environmental press—real institutional control, rigid structure, simple stimulation potential, discouragement of affect, strong impulse control.

Retarded adults in a sheltered workshop are a good example. They need a structured environment. They can be educated to do wondrous things in a relatively unvaried environment. However, a single change may upset everything. If a new person joins the group, there is excitement, individuals stop doing their tasks, and the agitation increases. All because one new person represents a quantum leap in the environmental press for these folks.

Persons of average competence can cope effectively with average environmental press. Persons of high competence can cope with a lot of environmental press, stimulation, responsibility, and change.

Adaptation fans out. Those with a low level of competence can only deal with a narrow range of variation in environmental press. The higher the level of competence, the greater the range of environmental press one can deal with. So, some days can be boring, some can be overwhelming and one can handle the variation.

a. Competence exceeds press. Unfortunately, for most of us there is not a perfect fit between competence and environmental press. Sometimes we are more competent than the press. In this case "passive" maladaptation is typical. A competent person may find himself in an environment that is fairly unvaried, unstimulating and predictable. But the brain needs stimulation to survive. Maladapted behaviors often result. For example, assembly line work can be boring and repetitious, with one's competence exceeding the environmental press. In this instance the person may become passively maladapted to such work, engaging in brain-stimulating diversions such as withdrawal, daydreaming, escape, fantasy, sabotage, all predictable consequences of the situation.

One of the earliest signs that a receptionist does not have a challenging enough environmental press may be that she is reading the newspaper or doing the crossword puzzle. Presumably the employer did not hire an incompetent person, but the job demands have gotten so repetitious and boring over time that environmental press has decreased. The employee looks for other stimulation. Absenteeism is another sure indicator.

Not all adaptive behavior will be as passive as daydreaming. More active forms of maladaption may include fault finding, making criticisms without ever following up. Competent people doing the same job over and over, such as riveters on the assembly line, may resort to sabotage, doing something mischievous to heighten their environmental press.

The average resident of a nursing home in the United States is a female, age 83, who has been in the facility ten years. The environment that remains the same will get weaker and weaker as a press for this individual. That resident's brain is programmed to survive, and the increasingly weak environment will encourage fantasizing and daydreaming. That's the signal that more environmental press is needed. In too many facilities the typical staff reaction to resident "confusion" is that there is one less person they have to worry about.

b. Press exceeds competence. When environmental press exceeds competence, there is likely to be a more "active" maladaptation. Acting-out behavior, aggression, anger, scapegoating, and abuse are likely to be the consequences. This does not necessarily mean that the persons involved are incompetent. They may be highly competent, but functioning in an environment where press exceeds competence.

Consider an example from the military. During REFORGER, a combined military training exercise for NATO troops, the demands of the environmental press become considerable. Skilled technicians running the machinery for air traffic control may have been trained, under ordinary circumstances, to handle five or ten planes in the air. Now, during these exercises, there may be twenty or thirty planes under their control. In consequence, the technicians act out. There may be anger, aggression, scapegoating. In all-male units there may be physical abuse; in all-female units, verbal abuse.

"Burn out" is a typical result of press exceeding competence. Burned-out workers are very angry people, especially in human services. They see themselves as having given their all and nothing happened. They feel they get no thanks, little recognition, and not enough pay for what they are doing.

Neglect and abuse are beginning to be recognized as the consequences of an overloaded staff. They may be the result when people who are too little recognized have just too much to do. It is being documented now that when whole wings of people are neglected, treated abruptly, verbally or physically abused, this may be conscious, or most likely, the unconscious consequence of this maladaptation.

5. Creative Environmental Press

Fortunately, the model is quite fluid. One fundamental principle is that, left to its own devices, environmental press will go from strong to weak. The first day on the job a new employee will be nervous. Six months later, if he still feels that way, something is wrong. The environmental press has become somewhat more routinized. The longer a person does the same thing, the weaker the environmental press becomes. What you find is that creative workers are constantly adding nuances to the job and assuming more responsibility, keeping mobile.

But sometimes people have a vested interest in staying adapted to an environment despite lessening environmental press. If this happens, as press decreases, so does the person's competence.

A resident in a facility may present an example of such a situation. Because the environment does not change substantially, the environmental press declines unless we intervene. However, the resident may have a heavy investment in staying adapted. He has no other place to go. He's not going to make waves. His competence declines further and further until it becomes practically non-existent.

As a staff person you must respond to the situation. What do you do? There are two alternatives. First, you can increase the range of what is considered tolerable adaptive behavior. Or second, you can increase the environmental press. Both these alternatives will increase competence.

a. The Activity Coordinator as Environmental Press. In the nursing home, the activity coordinator is a part of the environmental press. The changes that are made in the environment through activities can help to maintain the competence of the residents.

You will recall we said that competence is an aggregate with four components. If that is so, can it be that if we invest some more time in sensori-motor activities for our people, or if we can get people feeling better about themselves, there will be a spill-over effect so that health status or cognitive skills can be improved? Will activity coordinators be able to make changes in their areas of expertise and thereby change overall competence? I suspect the answer is yes, so long as we don't ignore any of the areas completely.

We tend to focus on physical well-being. Don't totally ignore other aspects. You cannot expect residents to maintain mental agility if there is never anything in your program that involves any cognitive process, any mental challenge. Ask yourself what kind of competence does the environmental press in my facility address?

Some creative ways of enhancing the environmental press for your facility include the following:

1. The National Council on the Aging Humanities Program. This is a diverse compilation of readings from literature with discussion questions and suggested projects relating to different themes. The program encourages reminiscense and a recognition of the humanities in elders' lives.

2. Hospital Satellite Network. This is a private TV network that has begun broadcasting high quality programming to hospital personnel and patients. Programming ten hours per day seven days a week includes two feature films each day, health maintenance for residents and staff, continuing education and special children's programs.

3. College/nursing home linkages. Community colleges are now offering such college-level courses as art, sociology, and language in nursing homes. The entire community is invited to participate, and the facility becomes a community focal point.

4. Intergenerational programming. Introduced with careful preparation of the children to be involved, this activity can be enlivening and mutually beneficial for children and elders.

5. Family involvement in programming and teaching. David Furse, in an article in the August 1983 issue of the *American Health Care Association Journal,* points out that successful care of a nursing home resident requires consideration of the triangle of resident, staff, and family. If any part of the triangle is neglected, the quality of care suffers.

CONCLUSION

It is important to remember that even though you as an activities professional are a very significant part of the resident's environmental press, you are not the entire press. Other residents, family, community are potentially "Not Me" for the resident. Use these resources to contribute to the resident's life satisfaction. Activities are a significant contribution to the residents' quality of life. You, with an understanding of environmental press, are vital to their maintenance and growth.

REFERENCES

Lawton, M.P. *Environment and aging.* Monterey, CA: Brooks/Cole Publishing Co., 1980.

Lawton, M.P. Competence, environmental press, and the adaptation of old people. In M.P. Lawton, P.G. Windley and T.O. Byerts (Eds.) *Aging and the environment: Theoretical approaches.* New York: Garland STPM Press, 1980.

Organizing a Men's Club*

Marian Bentel
Audrey Lasher

ABSTRACT. This article explains the needs and reasons for camaraderie among men patients. It describes the planning of a Men's Club, and it relates a number of successful programs. Also included are the values derived and the successes of the Men's Club.

REASONS AND NEEDS FOR A MEN'S CLUB

Five years ago the decision was made in the Activities Department of the United Methodist Home and Nursing Hospital to organize a Men's Club. Our facility has three levels of care and dwelling: The United Methodist Home and Cottages, The Intermediate Care Facility, The Skilled Nursing Unit. For some time it was evident that there was need for camaraderie among the men because they were greatly outnumbered by the women residents and patients. At that time the ratio was 6 to 1, and it has remained at the same ratio. Developing the Men's Club has proven to be challenging and rewarding because of its steady growth and the interest shown by our men. We were aware that some men had no interest in games or parties, and many men did not participate in any activity. For this reason, the club was formed to try to meet the continuing needs of our men. Its format resembles a service club. We patterned it after a service club as we felt that a number of the men could relate to this because of their former life style. The group meets once a month at 12 o'clock noon for luncheon and a program that follows.

Marian Bentel, B.A., is Remotivation Coordinator, and Audrey Lasher, O.T.R., is Director of Occupational Therapy and Activities at United Methodist Home and Nursing Hospital, 31 N. Park Avenue, Meadville, PA 16335.

*This article was not part of the Convention Program; however, it represents some of the submitted papers that were accepted for publication. In forthcoming journal issues you will be treated to other selections that, while not presented, were deemed worthy of promulgation by the NAAP Education Review Team.

PLANNING FOR MEETINGS

The Activity Department is the cohesive force behind the Men's Club and is responsible for planning and bringing the men together for their meetings. A great deal of planning precedes each meeting. Guest speakers and programs are carefully considered to maintain quality and variety in the meetings. The programs have included all facets of the community: business, clergy, local government, all forms of the arts, the local college, travel, and sports. It has been our goal to utilize the resources of the community in our facility, and for five years we have met with success.

The club meets on the same day each month, but a flyer is given out to each man which reminds him of the program and the date. The flyers are given to all Nurses Stations and put on bulletin boards throughout the facility. The flyer is a clever reminder sketched by an artistic member of our Activity Department, and it has attractive drawings to catch the eye and encourage attendance. A Certificate of Recognition is given at the close of the meeting to the speaker for the day, and this is beautifully printed by one of our employees. On the day itself a number of employees from all departments aid in transporting patients in wheelchairs and geriatric chairs to the Recreation Room for the meeting. We continue to be pleased with the attendance. We have nearly 100 percent from the men in the Home and Intermediate Care Facility and as many men who are physically able from the nursing unit. The membership has grown from an average of 20 men per meeting to 35 at each meeting.

The dietary staff has to be aware of the men who are attending in order to plan for any special diets. We have become increasingly conscious that a menu which appeals to the men is really an important motivation, and we notice the admiring glances at the dessert table as they gather for the meeting. Pie, for instance, is a great motivator. So, we must have pie! Some men happily remind us at every meeting that the food tastes much better at the Men's Club. Men's Club has become a special event, and even the food is looked forward to with anticipation by many of the men.

THE MEETINGS AND THEIR CONTENT

The meetings have consistently run very smoothly, and this is due primarily to the men who agree to accept the leadership for the day. Some of the men have been our master of ceremonies for a period of time. Others have agreed to give the invocation and others have introduced the guest speakers. Very recently we have included group singing which has been directed by one of our musically talented men. It has been a heart warming experience to hear all those male voices singing out such songs as, "Let Me Call You Sweetheart" and "Down By the Old Mill Stream."

Once a year a men's service club from our community joins with our men's club for a combined meeting. On two occasions our men were asked to join with the service club at their meeting place. What a pleasurable experience it was for our men to leave the facility and go out into the community. It is always a stimulating experience for our men to shake hands with men from the community and engage in discussing their former vocations, sports, hunting, politics and in general what is called "Men Talk." The memory of this event keeps our men talking and reminiscing for countless days.

We feel very proud of the programs which have been presented for the past five years. We can honestly say that in contacting the persons to give the programs we have not had one refusal. On many occasions they have expressed pleasure that our facility offers such a stimulating activity for men. Their pleasure is consistently evident in the stimulating and creative programs which they present. There have been a number of excellent programs, but we will list some that linger in the memories of the men:

1. Historical programs of John Brown and his involvement in the history of our local area.
2. Biographical sketches of former U.S. Presidents in celebration of Presidents Day.
3. Demonstration of throwing clay on potters wheel by local artists.
4. Nature slides taken personally by a professional photographer.
5. Musical program by concert pianist from local college.
6. Program on Pennsylvania State Forests by state forester.
7. True experiences with the American Indians of southwestern U.S. related by local college professor.
8. Paintings displayed by local artist and some techniques explained.
9. A unique collection of antique men's hats.
10. Pennsylvania's Master Farmer of 1975 explained his successful poultry farm business.

11. "The True Meaning of Armistice Day" presented by a local professor to celebrate Veterans' Day.
12. Christmas musical program given by local high school girl's choral group.
13. Informative talk on Mt. St. Helens given by local geologist.
14. "Western U.S.A.—A Touch of Yesterday and Today" a slide program by a local professor.
15. A dramatization of the life of a former local clown.
16. Local Philatelist displayed and talked about his collection.

It is important to relate that in several meetings we have utilized our own men and their talents to present programs. One of the men in conjunction with his wife showed slides and talked about their trip to the West. His pleasure in seeing his slides once more was quite obvious, and he exhibited such great pride as he relayed detail after detail regarding facts of the trip. Everyone enjoyed that day along with him. Another man showed a very professional film called "Wheels Across America"[1] in which he had taken an active part in preparing meals for a group of bicyclers as they traveled. Still another talented gentleman prepared a beautiful Christmas program of vocal music in which he sang and also led the men in singing Christmas carols. In these programs we have utilized our own members and their talents, and it has been successful.

Our desire has always been to encourage the men to feel an important part of the organization, yet not burdening them with too much responsibility. So if one of the men happens to be acquainted with the speaker, we encourage him to do the introduction. Also, on an occasion one of our men who is a sports fan and who previously had been a Big League baseball player, introduced a speaker who presented a timely talk on baseball and then shared his baseball memorabilia with the men. This introduction is one we will remember because he revealed such a clever sense of humor, and he related some humorous incidents from his own background.

VALUES OF MEN'S CLUB

Many programs of the Men's Club deal with timely topics and current events which help to expose the men to the outside world and its ever-changing society. We feel that the men coming together

---

[1]Wheels Across America, produced by Taylor University.

in the formation of a club helps to retain the men's sexual identity which can be important to their ego strength. The club has brought our men together in a relaxed atmosphere, and it has given them the opportunity to develop friendships with men from different areas of our facility. We have observed that when our men meet with the community service club they have the opportunity to experience pride and self worth once more as they talk of their former vocations and their past life. We feel meeting with other men can bring about a wholesome nostalgia of former days and former life styles. Our administration has been helpful in innumerable ways, but attending the meetings and interacting with the men has proved perhaps the most beneficial to them. Because of the continued interaction between our administration, the guest speakers from our community, and our men, we are convinced that our Men's Club is an excellent remotivational vehicle which can act as a bridge for the men to the outside world.

Art Therapy With the Institutionalized Older Adult*

Madeline M. Rugh

The image of aging and the aged in our society is a limited one that focuses upon detriments and aging as a disease, especially for older adults in institutions.

> When an older adult moves to a nursing home it has been found that there tends to be a marked change in self-conception, which includes a shift in thinking of oneself as progressively physically and mentally handicapped, from independent to dependent, from aspiring to declining. (Hurlock, 1959)

Aging is equated with death, something that happens to other people. We do not prepare for either event, even though both are inevitable. Nor do we have support systems for helping the aged make the necessary and very difficult adjustments to the physical, emotional and environmental changes they may face. "Old age is the period in life with the greatest number of profound crises, often occurring in multiples and with high frequency" (Butler, 1977).

Most assistance is geared toward maintenance of physical health which may aggravate the situation by prolonging life in an institution devoid or weak in providing opportunities for emotional and mental fulfillment. "There is evidence that most personality breakdowns in old age are not the results of brain damage but rather social conditions which give rise to feelings of insecurity" (Hurlock, 1959).

Madeline M. Rugh received her bachelor's degree in fine arts from Columbus College of Art and Design, Columbus, Ohio, and her Master's Degree in Art Education from the University of Michigan. Her address is 910 West Nebraska, Norman, Oklahoma 73069.

*This article was not part of the Convention Program; however, it represents some of the submitted papers that were accepted for publication. In forthcoming journal issues you will be treated to other selections that, while not presented, were deemed worthy of promulgation by the NAAP Education Review Team.

While it is true that older adults in nursing homes or extended care facilities account for only 4 or 5 percent of the population, that number jumps to 20 percent for the ages of 75 and over. One out of every five older adults will be hospitalized at some point. Whether their stay is brief, extended, or permanent, it is crucial that the experience be one of total health care including attention to residents' emotional well-being. Care must be taken to prevent the development of a dependent, declining, handicapped self-image which reinforces the current negative social image and serves as a poor model for aging. It is to this destructive imagery that art therapists, art educators and others from the humanities field have addressed themselves by developing programs that deal creatively and intelligently with the emotional and cognitive needs of individuals both in and out of institutions.

The following text is documentation of one such program that used the visual arts in a therapeutic/educational manner. The primary goal was to change not only the way the institutionalized older adult views himself/herself and his or her potential for continued growth and creative expression, but also the way others—staff, family and community—view their elders who have been hospitalized. The program was planned around the following therapeutic and educational objectives:

1. To foster greater awareness of self and environment, including reality orientation when necessary.
2. To promote feelings of pride and self-worth and to help develop a more positive self-image.
3. To develop skills required for expression in the visual arts.
4. To facilitate greater communication and socialization between residents, residents and staff, and the art program and the community.

It should be noted that I have paired therapeutic and educational goals. Where one of these two distinct approaches begins and the other leaves off is a controversial subject currently being debated and defined by art educators and art therapists. In this program that addresses an audience confined to the institution art therapy always precedes art education. The greatest problem encountered in bringing art experiences to *any* older adult is resistance. Resistance is based on fear—fear of making mistakes, a feared lack of skill due to previous negative art experiences, no previous art experience or years of built up notions and suppositions about the nature of art as something just for the gifted and talented. The basis of this fear is self-doubt. To enter into an art experience with an emphasis on technique and product to the exclusion of feelings and personal meaningfulness could fuel this fear and severely limit the number of people willing to participate in the art process. Art educators understand that self-concept is a critical factor in designing art programs for the older adult, yet they espouse programs that . . . "refuse to compromise the integrity of the art experience, true involvement with the arts can only come when an older person forms attitudes that recognize the arts as suitable and important intellectual opportunities . . . " (Hoffman, 1979).

There is an implied elitism here that would support many older persons' contention that art is just for the gifted. Art therapists have something to offer art educators at the point where a technical production orientation breaks down, not by abusing the arts but by beginning where the participant is developmentally and by expanding the parameters of what is acceptable. It is necessary . . . "to submerge the teacher personality and standards so that any fragile expression that shows its head will be tenderly cultivated and encouraged" (MacDonald, 1941).

In my opinion the key to successful involvement of an older adult in an art program does not rest with a sophisticated product but is contingent upon developing and sustaining a positive self-concept *whereby the adult comes to know, understand and appreciate his or her special view of the world and way of expressing that awareness.* For some, it is important to pay more attention to the art product after a lack of confidence is overcome. For others, who may have gained confidence but have severe physical or emotional disability, the therapists must maintain a balance. Respect and honor for all levels of artistic expression must be learned and maintained. "Every person born into this world represents something new, something that never existed before, something original and unique . . . Every single man is a new thing in the world and is called upon to fulfill his particularity in this world" (Moustakas, 1967).

The following section describes several participants in the art therapy program sponsored by Jackson Community College, Community Services Department, Norman, Oklahoma. Each description includes information about the physical condition, emotional/attitudinal state, cognitive development and the environment of the participant. Also included is information about the method of presenting art experiences, art education/art therapy components, materials used, and the development of individuals from the initial exposure to the last recorded expression.

PORTRAITS

An art therapy program sponsored by Jackson Community College's Community Services Department was begun in local nursing homes and extended care facilities in January 1980. Classes meet once a week for an hour and a half. The story of this program is available as a synchronized slide/tape presentation produced by the author in cooperation with the American Art Therapy Association, the University of Michigan School of Gerontology, and the University of Oklahoma Media Services Division. Persons interested in renting a copy can contact the author at the University of Oklahoma Counseling Center, Norman, Oklahoma, 73069.

Portraits 1 and 2: Art and Dan

Art and Dan have both been blind two or three years. Neither has received any help in learning to use other senses. As a result they have developed many behavioral problems and great negativity about their ability to do anything or be worth anything.

The late onset of sugar diabetes which caused Art's blindness also resulted in the loss of his legs from the knee down. He has little sensitivity in his hands and claims his left hand is totally numb. Despite the disabilities, Art is kind, has a mild sense of humor and sharp memory. He will try most anything. His most restrictive handicap is his sense of worthlessness.

Dan, a much heavier, more massive man, had a much more negative personality. He would sit in his room and masturbate, drooling and shouting unintelligibly. Very bitter about his condition, he allowed himself to reach a low level of disgust and despair. His attention span is short but he has mellowed since we first began and listens quietly. The staff did not allow him out of his room because they feared his inappropriate behavior. That restriction only perpetuated the negative behaviors. He has never masturbated nor wet his clothing when in art class.

It took nearly a year of experimentation to find the most effective media for these men. Contrary to what one might think, it was not something three-dimensional such as clay, though clay is used to help loosen the men's shoulders, elbows and wrists which were extremely stiff. Dan had been a stone mason. Art worked in a factory, but his father had been a stone mason.

We began with motivations centering around their personal experiences—tearing clay into "rock" shapes to build a stone wall or bridge between the men. Dan showed a sensitivity not previously seen when he inquired about Art's legs being amputated. Later Dan made a clay shape of a pet skunk he once had. Dan had good use of his hands. They were very sensitive, but he usually just squeezed the clay or smeared it. Art could not use both hands so shaping was more difficult. We turned to drawing as a last resort.

We focused on mental images from the past or of things very familiar to both men. Their hands drew what they saw with their "mind's eye." A paper and marker that squeaked were immediately more successful than the constructing. (Apparently, the mental image translates into two-dimension more readily or easily than three-dimension. More research needs to be done in this area.)

Although both men continued to express negative feelings about the drawing exercise, they were usually quiet and attentive while working. They could not see what they had done, but they had a sense of the kinesthetic action or process. A bonus of positive reinforcement came from others who could recognize the drawing shapes better than the clay shapes. Their self-portraits were very successful. Dan's portrait had sharp teeth and an angry expression. When he was told about this he actually laughed for the first time in a year. Art's portrait had big ears and disheveled hair and glasses just like him. He laughed when we described the ears and hair.

The art work was mounted and hung in each man's room to stimulate continual reinforcement from visitors and staff. We are continuing to explore this media despite attitudinal resistance from both men. It will take a great deal of time to overcome their loss of self-esteem.

Portrait 3: In Memory of Ethel, Lillian, Olive, Alice and Kathryn

All of the above women have died since the beginning of the art program. Ethel was blind, and Lillian had Parkinson's Disease. The others were in the nursing home because they had suffered strokes.

The strength of spirit and will they exhibited just prior to death supports McLeish's contention that anyone can have the strength of will to live and to die creatively.

Ethel was a skittish small woman with tiny features and a high trembling voice. She told vivid stories of her past, of the bean factory, farm animals, the milk cart drawn by a horse. A victim of cataracts without money to have them removed, she retreated into a dark world and became fearful, shaky and emotional. Unlike the men that were blind, Ethel worked well in clay, probably due to her patience and careful use of her hands. She created a barn full of animals which she displayed proudly in her room. She maintained a wonderful sense of humor despite her fears. In the short time I had with her, she showed tenacity if encouraged and was able to problem-solve and act independently of me.

Her fears grew to the point where she could not bear to be alone and called out constantly. She received medication which only contributed to the problem. We made an attempt to help her find relief from her fears by playing soothing music and having her create with the clay the things she was feeling. This had only a temporarily calming effect.

Lillian was a very interesting woman in her late seventies. Though toothless and with a wobbling head and hands that resulted from Parkinson's Disease, she was able to walk and converse with great agility. She had a rather deep voice but was quiet and uncertain. The shaking in her hands created a lively line when she painted. Many older adults are dismayed by their shaking hands. It is important to point out the beauty in a varied line and then reinforce that opinion as legitimate by showing slides of professional artists' works that employ a more expressive line. Lillian displayed an unusual early developmental level in her art, a combination of fold-out perspective and x-ray perspective. Sometimes it was difficult to understand the images because of this but they formed strongly decorative patterns on paper.

We began working on a one-to-one basis until she could be convinced to join a group. This is a good way to reach people in a nursing home who might otherwise never volunteer or attempt to participate in a group activity. Motivation stemmed from conversation with her about her life in Kentucky, sometimes inspired by looking through a book of landscapes.

After trying several media, she selected watercolor which we used in an experimental sense rather than in a professional sense.

She began painting simple flowers and moved on to complicated subjects—caves that she had explored, a violent storm with uprooted trees she had experienced, the woodburning stove, table and tea cup, etc.

She was very timid at first and lacked confidence. The last major thing she completed before her death was a coal bucket made of clay that even had little pieces of coal inside. She was very proud of it and selected her own colors and completed it without any coaxing. When her relatives came to take her body back to Kentucky, they were amazed and excited by her art work and took several pieces with them to remember her by.

Olive, a stroke victim, had lost the use of her left arm and experiences acute visual trouble. A gentle woman with a quiet delicate manner, she was unable to control a slight drool. She had painted as a young woman and worked independently, needing only some technical assistance and lots of encouragement. She was dismayed by her shaking hand. Since she was painting a landscape, we noted that lines in nature are rarely straight. She smiled at this and continued on. Upon finishing one picture she noted the house was leaning. Some of the other students, in keeping with my tradition of finding a reason for everything, told her it was probably a very windy day. Everyone chuckled at this and it was settled. Olive finished two major paintings which she worked at continuously, completing the last just two days prior to going into a coma that preceded her death.

Alice, a former pianist whose long bony fingers were lined with blue vessels, seemed so frail, but she was perfectly alert. Her shallow cheeks always held a smile. She was not sure she could do anything in art but was willing to try. Those who are very together people often have a need to produce very controlled pieces; this is always acknowledged and accepted. Once they realize that they are still in control, they will venture into the more risky affairs. Alice was one such woman. We decided on a tissue paper collage. She enjoyed the delicate operation required by very careful placement. Surprised and delighted by the completed piece, she came up with her own ideas for future works.

Though still in the very "practical" vein, we found ways for her to be more creative and challenging. For example, she had an important picture she wanted framed. It was suggested that she design a frame for it using the collage technique she had acquired skill in.

The last time I saw her, she could not remember where she was and was continually losing contact with the present. She had great difficulty organizing images but she tried very hard to finish her picture. Soon after, she died. Her art work was also treasured by her relatives.

Kathryn was a large, overweight woman with big brown eyes that were a blend of gentleness and pain. At first she came timidly to the art therapy class and drew a safe picture of flowers. She was asked to add more detail, to think of where the flowers might be located. She elaborated and created a very detailed, sensitive piece. She worked independently, needing only emotional support and encouragement. She came even when the dark circles under her eyes reflected her increasing pain. One day I observed her working ceaselessly, showing an intensity I had not seen before. I was struck by this and intuitively felt she would soon die. Her drawing, of the interior of her home as a child, was complete with details like cups on the shelves and a mouse in the corner. When this work was finished, she became very ill and was bedridden until her death.

These women all displayed tremendous concentration and made valiant efforts to complete their art work just prior to death. This is certainly a subject for further research. One may take comfort in the idea that perhaps the completion of these paintings was a most humane and triumphant completion of their unique beings.

Portrait 4: Burl

"You do this, make a picture, and the first thing you know something else comes to mind and you can talk about it." From Burl I learned the importance of the art as a vehicle for communication between people and as a message from the self. Many older adults, especially those in nursing homes, are isolated from each other, partly because of physical impairments that make communication a difficult affair and partly because of the introspective nature of aging. Art becomes a bridge between people. For Burl, a large red-faced man of Swedish descent, this bridging gave him great pleasure. He looked forward to completing his work, for this helped him maintain a sense of time.

Although many people feel that the art experience should be completed in one session, it has been my observation that working in-depth on something week after week is a more meaningful and comfortable method for older adults. They look forward to coming to class to be with an old friend or visit a place in their picture from their past that was pleasant. In the case of those who have died, the creative act may even have postponed death or great illness. There is research indicating an association between creative activity and longevity (Dawson and Baller, 1972).

Burl is 77 years old and suffers from brain tumors for which he has had several major operations. He creates paintings and clay reliefs of images from his past in a charming folk-art style all his own. The director of this facility, understanding the necessity for a display area, erected a large display unit and even gave it a name in large letters. He called it the "Life Gallery." For the opening of this art gallery, Burl designed the invitation of which he was extremely proud and spoke of fondly several months later. Burl always tells me how the gallery gives people an opportunity to talk together. It is a constant reminder to staff and relatives that these people are interesting, humorous, intelligent, creative human beings.

Portrait 5: Gladys

"It takes the pain away." So says a 91-year-old lady of great refinement. (That characteristic does not stop her from making up songs about the elevator when we're riding in it!) Gladys is not stuffy but a real perfectionist, very demanding of herself and others. The staff is calling her another Grandma Moses. Petite, witty and very serious about her art work, she is an elderly prodigy. Although she never drew before in her life, she became very involved after a brief but stormy introduction to art and now carries a sketch pad and pencils with her.

We began the usual way by determining what media or materials she preferred. Very negative at first, she demanded that I show her exactly how I would draw it. I weasled out of this demand by conveying my confidence in her and in her human capacity to create. Still pressing me to do it for her, I mentioned that there is no right or wrong way, that it was impossible for me to determine *how* she as a unique individual should draw. She must discover that for herself. Needless to say, she was very angry with me and grudgingly completed what she had started. (Her ability was obvious to me even in a few marks, so my decision not to give in to her pleas was reinforced.)

Soon she was amazed at what she had done, and I told her she should be proud that she had done it all herself. The work reflected great intelligence and courage. Gladys was sold! She laughed and said, "You're some teacher. I really did do that myself, didn't I? I never knew I could draw!" She draws in her room now during the week. Recently she told me, "I used to just look out of my window, now I can see."

Portrait 6: Millie

Millie was an attractive woman in her middle seventies, able to walk but with speech and visual impairment as the result of a stroke. Millie expressed great anxiety over art, claiming as most do that she couldn't draw, that she had no skill, that she was dumb and that young people didn't like old people anyway. Not being able to communicate is a devastating thing, for the implication is that one is stupid if one cannot talk well. It was necessary to explain to her over and over that the stroke damaged her speech, but had not affected her intelligence. Art as a bridge to facilitate more effective or alternative communication forms is of vital importance to a woman like Millie. Predictably she was highly critical of her art work, but the examination of different art styles and the strengths in her own work have helped considerably.

Probably the most important and most frequently repeated statement in my art sessions is that art is like you or your signature—unique, special. There will never be anyone who sees quite your way or who has experienced what you have. Consequently, each person will express himself/herself in a unique and different way. No right or wrong, good or bad, just you. A teacher can never let a negative comment slip by. Such comments are always calls for help and support. Repetition of these concepts of uniqueness is critical to the establishment and maintenance of an art program in a nursing home.

Very slowly Millie gained more confidence while at the same time her work improved. She seemed more comfortable, teasing, joining and interacting with other students in a supportive way. Once there is a spark of interest a teacher must fan it, not by lying or patronizing, but by being prepared to make the most of any positive occurrence, no matter how minute. This requires flexibility and quick thinking. This is MacDonald's "submerging of the teacher personality." It took a full year and a half to light Millie's fire. She was recently the first place winner of a senior citizen art contest.

When she received the check for $100, she kissed it and said, "It's unbelievable!"

Portraits 7 and 8: Saul and Mary

Saul and Mary have been grouped together because they both felt less creative than the other students; they were unable to make "real" pictures. Mary's were linear and Saul's were massive shapes. It is interesting to note that many, many older adults use lines and outlines for objects and very seldom "fill in" the shapes or forms with solid color. When asked to add color, fill in or color in, etc., they seemed perplexed and usually added more lines to the outlines. Collage and paint sometimes alter this propensity. (This may relate to perceptual damage from stroke, or perhaps it reflects a psychological condition. This is a definite area for further investigation.) Mary and Saul were shown pictures of modern art to help them find value in their work. The values of lines and shapes were discussed as conveyors of essence and emotion. After all, "Representation is not the aim of art, what one should look for is the vitality of the imaginative life of the individual—seeing by means of the "inner eye." (Collier, 1977).

Or as Rudolf Arnheim has observed, "[historically speaking] . . . abstract styles of representation have prevailed—*not as preparatory steps on the road to something more perfect but as the fully materialized, adequate expression of certain conceptions of life and functions of art in life*" (Arnheim, 1966). [Italics mine.]

This is an extremely important concept, especially for older adults like Mary and Saul. As Robert Butler has hypothesized, the form and content of the creative expression for this end of the life-cycle may be different but still be "perfect and fully materialized expression." We must find out what the nature of this expression is and convey that to the older adults who cannot see their own beauty and worth.

Mary was almost on the verge of tears over this issue. It was not until she had seen her work framed and hung that she began to understand and appreciate what she had made. During the opening of our art gallery she was beaming. A very quiet woman with Parkinson's Disease, she has become much more at ease with her work. Incidentally, she has made representational forms but she loses contact with what they are, completing the piece *despite* the image.

Recently, we tried an art stitchery project for which she drew the image. It will be interesting to see if she can follow through, maintaining awareness of the shape through completion. This might indicate that the choice of media is having an effect on her representational ability.

Saul is 70 years old and has been institutionalized all his life for childhood paralysis. The only things he had ever done prior to our art class was to stuff "monkeys" with sponge. He is ecstatic with his new-found abilities. Hunched over in his chair with deformed feet and extreme visual impairment, he labors just an inch above his paper. We noticed that his art work resembled stained glass church windows and have invented a way of displaying and mounting them to make the most of their brilliant colors. He never misses class but still requires verbal support and encouragement though he is largely independent—probably for the first time in his life.

Portrait 9:
Dena

Slightly balding, her thin hair frames a pale face with shy but observant blue eyes. She is a deaf/mute who has never attended school nor been taught how to communicate. Her art work is outstanding. We began by experimenting with several media and looking at found objects. We made motions and faces to indicate textures and patterns. She followed the shapes with her finger and then drew following the contour she had just traced. Her early work was primitive but structurally accurate. She used simple forms without much detail and has progressed to larger somewhat more complicated pieces.

Changing the material for drawing has helped her achieve more diversity, but she still maintains her striking simplicity. She is extremely pleased with her work, for it is the first way in which she has communicated in an effective manner. Her art work shows that she is strong, bold, intelligent, and a very sensitive, special human being.

Portrait 10:
"The Back Ward"

In most nursing homes or extended care facilities, there is a unit that houses those who are disoriented to a crippling point and those who are violent, angry and unresponsive. These people have emotional turmoil coupled with disabling strokes and other crises which have befallen them. They have very low feelings of self-esteem and are therefore a real challenge to involve in the art experience. Once they have made an effective "mark," their tolerance for themselves and their "condition" becomes more flexible. They begin to see themselves with fresher vision, as capable, unique and interesting people. These people should not be forgotten; they can benefit tremendously from an art therapy program. The worst "condition" that one can readily see is the loss of identity, of a sense of self and self-respect. The art product provides a concrete, permanent record that they exist, they they have something to say, that they are somebody. The class schedule provides a time reference to help with reality awareness. One woman who scribbled in circles and never seemed to know where she was or what was going on asked me if I was coming back next Friday. I was shocked. She then proceeded to remind me to bring her picture back and hang it.

Unfortunately, an insensitive staff person removed all the art work and threw it away. The result was devastating. Everyone forgot that he or she could do something. Those who were more oriented were hurt and asked why their work had been thrown away. This act of removing the art work said to these people what their predicament had been saying: you are not valued, what you do and who you are is unimportant. This has since been remedied and the long process of building self-esteem has begun again.

The method is two-fold. First we stimulate reminiscence of past experiences as subject matter. This may be done by showing slides or films, books or objects, but mainly is effected through listening and soliciting conversation. Secondly we try, immediately after the stimulus, to capture some essence of each person's reaction or remembrance. Both finished and unfinished work is hung at the end of the hour and talked about casually. Each week a piece is taken down if it is not done, and more detail is added until it is complete. In this way we maintain a sequence that grows slowly more complex, more challenging, more satisfying.

People of any age, when treated with respect, will eventually return the respect. These people are very kind to me, often eager to try more expressive experiences than their healthier contemporaries. To answer McLeish's query:

> Is there ever creativity in the survival of self over senility? Is it possible that this "I" so encircled by "disgust and despair" that its terrible urge is to take flight into somnolence and ex-

> tinction of the failed and rejected self, nonetheless creatively maintains its own existence and identity?'' (McLeish, 1976)

Based on my experience with the residents of the back ward, I answer an unqualified Yes!

Not included in the portraits are the younger groups encountered in nursing homes and extended care facilities. There are 40- and 50-year-old victims of multiple sclerosis who are very dedicated and effective art students. There are groups of 19- and 20-year-olds who have suffered brain damage from accidents or birth defects who are anxious to participate. The older adults are very supportive, compassionate and soothing mentors for the younger people, admiring their courage and sensitive to their suffering.

CONCLUSIONS

The need for more research in the area of old age and artistic, creative expression is evident. There are many questions yet to be answered or even posed. Are there stages of creative growth with the older adult that differ from those of children or adolescents? If so, what special needs or demands must be met to help the older adult grow in visual expression? As Butler suggests, does creativity in relation to different stages in the life cycle have a different form and content? What is the relationship, if any, between creative activity and longevity? What of the older adults perceptual style and how is this affected by depression, stroke, senile dementia?

These are just some of the many questions yet to be confronted by art educators, art therapists, psychologists, and sociologists working in the gerontological field.

In this paper, I have attempted to describe ways in which a visual arts program might help tap the creative potential of older adults confined to nursing homes. It has been demonstrated that there is a capacity within the elderly for creative expression and that the art process can actualize this potential for a wide range of people, provided a flexible framework is used. Maintaining an elitist attitude about art and art work will only deter full participation.

> Perhaps the arts have been prevented in our time from fulfilling their most important function by being honored too much. They have been lifted out of the context of daily life, exiled by exultation, imprisoned by awe-inspiring treasure-houses . . . .

works of art are not the whole of art . . . art is a . . . universal effort to give visible form to all aspects of life." (Arnheim, 1969)

Art with the older adult lies at the interface of art education and art therapy, requiring a humane interaction of both, for . . . "The ultimate goal is to discover how to permit elderly men and women to achieve in our time, and to live with a personal sense of wholeness and identity with which to grow toward their extinction." (O'Connor, 1979).

REFERENCES

Aplaugh, P. K., Renner, J. T., Birren, J. F. "Age and Creativity: Implications for Education and Teachers," *Educational Gerontology,* 1 (1), 1976.

Arnheim, Rudolf. *Toward a Psychology of Art.* Berkeley: University of California Press, 1966.

Arnheim, Rudolf. *Visual Thinking.* Berkeley: University of California Press, 1969.

Arnstine, Donald. "Art Education and The Economic Transformation of the Future," *Journal of Aesthetic Education,* 13 (2), April 1979.

Botwinick, Jack. *Aging and Behavior.* New York: Springer Publishing Co., 1973.

Butler, Robert, and Lewis, Myrna. *Aging and Mental Health.* St. Louis: C.V. Mosby Co., 1977.

Butler, Robert. "The Destiny of Creativity in Later Life: Studies of Creative People and the Creative Process" in *Psychodynamic Studies on Aging: Creativity, Reminiscing and Dying* by Ralph Kahana, Sidney Levin. New York: International University Press, 1967.

Collier, Graham A. "The Origins of Creativity," *Environments, Creativity and Aging,* Proceedings of the Fourth Annual Georgia Conference on Aging, May 1977.

Demner, Amy Caplan. "Techniques of Group Art Therapy for the Elderly in a Psychiatric Hospital Setting," *New York State Art Teachers Association Bulletin.* 29 (3), May 1979.

Dennis, Wayne. "Creative Productivity Between the Ages of 20 and 80 Years," *Journal of Gerontology,* 21, 1966.

Dewdney, Irene. "An Art Therapy Program for Geriatric Patients" in *Art Therapy: In Theory and Practice.* New York: Schocken Books, 1977.

Eisner, Elliot W. *Educating Artistic Vision.* New York: MacMillan Publishing Co., 1972.

Engel, Martin. "Some Helpful Hints for Teaching the Arts SERIOUSLY," *Art Education,* 34 (2), March 1981.

Farrah, Jere. *Arts and Aging an Agenda for Action.* Jacqueline T. Sunderland. Washington, D.C.: National Council on Aging, 1977.

Fischer, Trudy, Roe, Joan, and Fischer, Roland. "Creativity and Brain Damage," Proceedings of the Seventh Annual Conference of the American Art Therapy Association, October 1976.

Gardner, Howard. *Artful Scribbles.* New York: Basic Books, 1979.

Glick, Ruth. "Growing Wise about Growing Old" in *Education: An Arts/Aging Answer.* Washington, D.C.: National Council on Aging, 1979.

Harrison, Cynthia L. "Therapeutic Art Programs Around the World XIII: Creative Arts for Older People in the Community," *American Journal of Art Therapy,* 19 (4), July 1980.

Hass, Glen, Wiles, Kimball, and Roberts, Arthur. *Readings in Secondary Teaching.* Boston: Allyn & Bacon, Inc., 1970.

Hodnett, Mary Lee, Ph.D. "The Role and Scope of Art as Therapy Within the Art Education

Milieu,'' Invitational paper presented to the National Art Education Association. St. Louis, Mo., April 14, 1976.

Hoffer, Eric. ''Man, Play and Creativity,'' *Think*, 33(5), September/October 1967.

Hoffman, Donald H., ''The Elderly, The Arts and Individual Expression,'' *New York State Art Teachers Association Bulletin*, 29(3), May 1979.

Hoffman, Donald H. *Pursuit of Arts Activities with Older Adults: An Administrative and Programmatic Handbook.* University of Kentucky: Council on Aging, 1980.

Hoffman, Donald H. ''Stimulating the Elderly to Explore the Arts,'' *Art Education*, 38(4), April 1977.

Hoffman, Donald H., Greenberg, Pearl, and Fitzner, Dale. *Lifelong Learning and the Visual Arts: A Book of Readings.* National Arts Education Association, 1980.

Hurlock, Elizabeth B. *Developmental Psychology.* New York: McGraw-Hill Book Co., 1959.

Jennings, Ann S. ''Universities and the Arts: A Whole life Approach,'' *Art Education*, 38(4), April 1977.

Jones, Jean Ellen. *Teaching Art to Older Adults: Guidelines and Lessons.* Georgia State University, 1980.

Jungels, Georgiana. ''Cultural/Historical Considerations in Working with Older Clients in Art Therapy,'' *New York State Art Teachers Association Bulletin*, 29(3), May 1979.

Kimmel, D. C. *Adult and Aging: An Interdisciplinary Developmental View.* Somerset, New York: John Wiley and Sons, Inc., 1974.

Kogan, Nathan. ''Creativity and Cognitive Style: A Life-Span Perspective'' in *Life-Span Developmental Psychology* by Paul B. Baltes and K. Warner Schaie. Academic Press, 1973.

Lansing, Kenneth M. ''Art as a Humanizing Agent,'' *Art Education*, 31(8), December 1978.

Lehman, Harvey C. *Age and Achievement.* Princeton University Press, 1953.

Lupe, Anastasia. ''Art as Therapy in a Senior Citizen Center,'' *New York State Art Teachers Association Bulletin*, 29(3), May 1979.

Lytton, Hugh. *Creativity and Education.* New York: Schocken Books, 1972.

MacDonald, Rosabell. *Art as Education—Study of Art in the Secondary Schools.* Henry Holt & Co., 1941.

McLeish, John A. B. *The Ulyssean Adult: Creativity in the Middle and Later Years.* New York: McGraw-Hill Ryerson Ltd., 1976.

Mobley, Jane. ''She Doesn't Feel Bad Anymore,'' *Kansas City Star Weekly Magazine*, November 9, 1980.

Moustakas, C. E. *Creativity & Conformity.* New York: Van Nostrand Reinhold, 1967.

O'Connor, Francis V. ''Albert Berne and the Completion of Being: Images of Vitality and Extinction in the Last Paintings of a Ninety-six Year Old Man,'' in *Aging, Death and the Completion of Being* by David D. Van Tassel. Philadelphia, University of Pennsylvania Press, 1979.

Okin, M. A., DiVesta, F. J. ''Cautiousness in Adulthood as a Function of Age and Instructions,'' *Journal of Gerontology*, 31(5), 1976.

Peavy, R. Vance. ''Therapy and Creativity: A Dialogue,'' *Journal of Creative Behavior*, 13(1), 1979.

Romaniuk, Jean Gasen. ''Creative Thinking in Action: Reactions to a Workshop Designed for Older Adults,'' *Journal of Creative Behavior*, 12(4), 1978.

Rowan, Helen. ''The Creative People: How to Spot Them,'' *Think*, 28(10), November/December, 1962.

Rubin, Judith A. *Child Art Therapy.* New York: Van Nostrand Reinhold Co., 1978.

Scherer, Elisa Eisenman. ''The Integration of Art Therapy with Art Education,'' *New York State Art Teachers Association Bulletin*, 28(3), May 1978.

Torrance, E. Paul. ''Creativity and Futurism in Education: Retooling,'' *Education*, 100, Summer 1980.

Ulman, Elinor. ''Art Education for the Emotionally Disturbed,'' *American Journal of Art Therapy*, 17, October 1977.